LOS ANGELES Classic DESSERTS

LOS ANGELES *Classic* DESSERTS

Recipes from Favorite Restaurants

GRACE BAUER

PELICAN PUBLISHING COMPANY

GRETNA 2010

ISBN 9781589807815
Edited by Gene Bourg and Christine Ziemba

Layout based on a design by Kit Wohl

Printed in China
Published by Pelican Publishing Company, Inc.
1000 Burmaster Street, Gretna, Louisiana 70053

Dedicated to the sweet memory of my Grandmother,
Grace Moody Smith

CONTENTS

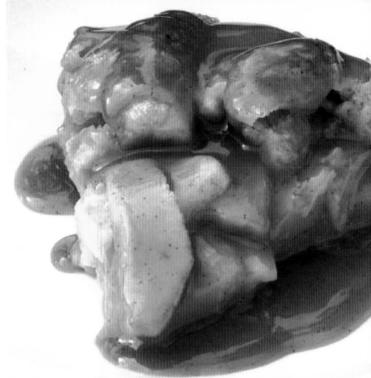

PREFACE

I am one of seven children. So my mother and grandmother (who owned and operated restaurants) had a lot of hungry mouths to feed every day. Dining out or relying on fast food was not an option – but dessert was always a grand part of the family meal, and it was a favorite of mine.

Pleasure and business brought me to Los Angeles many times, but the circumstances of Hurricane Katrina sent me here from New Orleans to Los Angeles to live, as well as attend culinary school and begin a new career. After I graduated, test cooking recipes for cookbooks became a sensual pleasure.

The task of choosing desserts to include from the second-largest city in the United States – and the 13th largest metropolitan area in the world – was somewhat daunting. With this book, I tried to provide a little glimpse into what Los Angeles has to offer in its panoply of cultural backgrounds and diverse tastes.

This book of dessert recipes includes some from famous Los Angeles restaurants that are no longer in existence, such as the Brown Derby and Chasen's and the Los Feliz Inn. The memory of them is indelibly etched in the minds of a multitude of Angelenos.

The book also includes recipes from other well-known dessert creators such as LaBrea Bakery, Sweet Lady Jane and Big Sugar Bakeshop. These are the go-to places for those who crave superior desserts.

Test-cooking desserts can be particularly challenging. In general, good cooking results from the right attitude and a comprehensive knowledge of ingredients. But baking is more science than art or intuition, and knowledge of ingredients will only take you so far. Dashes of this and pinches of that or such phrases as "to taste" are expressions not found in the baking world.

Every recipe in this book has been reviewed, tested, converted for serving size and modified as necessary for clarity and simplicity. I've attempted to make sure that directions are written clearly and comprehensively. Many recipes were tested more than once to assure accuracy.

One of my aims in writing this book was to reflect the Los Angeles melting pot of ethnicities and some of the city's cultural history. Writing it was also a delicious labor of love.

– *Grace Bauer*

It was indeed a glorious day in 2003 when master chef Joachim Splichal opened Patina in the spectacular Frank Gehry-designed Disney Concert Hall in Downtown Los Angeles. Splichal is considered one the premier chefs in the United States and his charming, playful and yet perfectly achieved culinary style complements the whimsical design of the Gehry creation beautifully.

Patina serves the best of California's seasonal ingredients, meaning the menu is ever changing and expanding, treating customers to new experiences time after time. Splichal's art lies in the creativity of his dishes. Though he has created a group of 11 restaurants, it is the original one, Patina, that is most loved by Angelenos.

His awards from the James Beard foundation include "Best California Chef" in 1991 and membership in "Who's Who of Food and Beverage in America" in 1995. He was recognized as a "Treasure of Los Angeles" in 1996 by the Central City Association and Los Angeles Mayor Richard Riordan.

Joachim works alongside his wife Christine who complements his culinary skills with her management and business expertise.

PATINA, CHEF JOACHIM SPLICHAL

CHOCOLATE MARCONA GATEAU

WITH CORPORATE EXECUTIVE CHEF ALAIN VERGNAULT, PATINA PASTRY

Most desserts are sweet and delicious. Some are unusual and fruity. Occasionally you'll find an especially satisfying one. But only rarely will you have one that actually brings you to your knees. This is the one!

YIELD: ONE 11-INCH CAKE, 6 TO 8 SERVINGS

1 1/2 cup	marcona almonds	1/8 teaspoon	vanilla extract
1 cup	granulated sugar, divided	half of 1/8 teaspoon	almond extract
7 ounces	dark chocolate, 64% cacao	crème fraîche	for garnish
3/4 cup, plus 2 tablespoons	unsalted butter		fresh blueberries, strawberries or blackberries for garnish
5 large	eggs		

Preheat oven to 400°F.

Butter an 11-inch round cake mold.

Medium chop the almonds. Place almonds in small mixing bowl an mix with 1/2 cup of the sugar.

In a double boiler, melt the chocolate and butter. Stir until well blended.

Place the eggs in a mixing bowl with the remaining 1/2 cup of sugar, vanilla extract and almond extract. Whisk the egg mixture for 5 minutes until it thickens. Fold the almonds into the mixture, then fold in the blended chocolate and butter. Pour the resulting mixture into the cake mold. Cook for 10 minutes at 400°F then lower oven temperature to 335°F and bake until a skewer inserted into the center comes out clean, about 35 – 40 minutes. Let the mixture cool completely, then remove it from the pan.

For serving, place a dollop of crème fraîche on top of each gateau along with fresh, seasonal berries. Vanilla ice cream or berry sorbet complements the heat of summertime and crème fraîche and powdered sugar are perfect for fall tastings.

BROWN DERBY

GRAPEFRUIT CAKE

Here is one of the old Brown Derby's classic desserts. Founded in 1926, the restaurant was very popular with Hollywood's most glamorous actors during the heyday of such stars as Clark Gable, Bette Davis and Lana Turner.

In this recipe, the addition of crushed grapefruit to the frosting, as well as having grapefruit sections placed between and on top of the cake, offer a promise of what's within.

YIELD: ONE 9-INCH CAKE

CAKE

1 1/2 cups	cake flour		1/4 cup	vegetable oil
3/4 cup	granulated sugar		3 large	eggs, separated
1 1/2 teaspoons	baking powder		4 tablespoons	fresh grapefruit juice
1/2 teaspoon	salt		1/2 teaspoon	lemon zest
1/4 cup	water		1/4 teaspoon	cream of tarter

Preheat oven to 350°F.

Sift together flour, sugar, baking powder and salt into mixing bowl. Make a well in center of dry ingredients. Into the well add the water, oil, egg yolks, grapefruit juice and lemon zest. Beat everything until very smooth. In another mixing bowl beat the egg whites and cream of tartar separately until the whites are stiff but not dry. Gradually pour the egg yolk mixture over whites and, with a rubber spatula, fold them together gently until they are just blended. Do not stir mixture.

Pour the mixture into an ungreased pan and bake 30 - 40 minutes, or until the cake springs back when lightly touched with a finger. Invert the cake on a rack. With the cake remaining in the pan, allow it to cool. Then run a spatula around edge of cake and carefully remove it from the pan. With a serrated knife, gently cut cake in half horizontally to create two layers.

GRAPEFRUIT CREAM CHEESE FROSTING

12 ounces	cream cheese		3 tablespoons	crushed grapefruit
2 teaspoons	fresh lemon juice		3 – 4 drops	yellow food coloring
1 teaspoon	grated lemon zest		2 cups	well drained
3/4 cup	powdered sugar, sifted			grapefruit sections

Allow the cream cheese to soften at room temperature, then beat until it is fluffy. Add the lemon juice and zest. Gradually blend in the sugar. Add the food coloring and beat the mixture until everything is well blended.

Crush a sufficient amount of grapefruit flesh to fill 2 tablespoons and blend them into the frosting. Spread some of the frosting on the bottom layer of the cake and top with grapefruit sections. Place the second layer atop the first and spread more frosting on the top and sides until they are covered. Garnish with the remaining grapefruit sections.

Recipe courtesy of Brown Derby

Of the many icons of Hollywood's Golden Era, the Brown Derby restaurant took its place as one of the stars' favorites. It was known for the hundreds of caricatures of Hollywood celebrities that filled its walls as well as well as for its novel architecture. The Brown Derby proved that you could build a restaurant anywhere – even in the shape of a hat – and if the food and service were good, the customers would come flocking.

Wonderful food, fine service and glamorous patrons brought international fame to the restaurant, a watering hole for such personalities as Frank Sinatra, Bob Hope, Jimmy Stewart, Lucille Ball, Gloria Swanson and Cecil B. DeMille.

At the time it was designed and built in 1926, fine dining in Los Angeles was still lacking. The Brown Derby helped change this. It embodied the California spirit of finest ingredients, great seasonings and plush comfort. In the Brown Derby pastry kitchen, the pastry chefs used only the purest and most expensive ingredients to make the cakes light, fluffy and delicious. They never tasted as they worked. Instead, they carefully measured and prepared ingredients knowing the finished product would come out perfectly.

This grapefruit cake was a favorite of the chefs as well as the guests who frequented the restaurant.

The Brown Derby restaurant closed in 1985.

(Continued from right)

Divide the ganache into two equal parts. Add the corn syrup to one half and set this aside. Fill a large bowl three-quarters full with ice water and place the bowl of remaining ganache in the ice bath to cool. Stir over the ice water, using a rubber spatula, until the ganache is thick.

Place one piece of the meringue in a serving platter and spread the cool ganache over it in an even layer. Top with another sheet of meringue.

WHIPPED CREAM FILLING

1 cup	heavy cream
1/2 cup	crème fraîche
1 tablespoon	granulated sugar

Combine the heavy cream and crème fraîche with the sugar and beat until fairly stiff. Spread in a thick, even layer over the second sheet of meringue. Top with the last sheet of meringue.

Stir the glaze, and if it has cooled too much to pour freely, heat it at 50 percent power in a microwave for 25 seconds. Pour the glaze over the top layer to drip down the sides.

Set aside the marjolaine and allow the glaze to cool and set. If you wish, trim the edges with a serrated knife.

Your marjolaine is now ready to slice with a serrated knife and serve. If you're not serving right away, cover it and store in the refrigerator.

WOLFGANG PUCK
MARJOLAINE

A marjolaine is created by stacking a series of hazelnut-flavored meringues separated by sweetened whipped cream. It's served chilled, sometimes with fruit. This recipe is from chef Wolfgang Puck's cookbook *Wolfgang Puck Makes it Easy*, published by Rutledge Hill Press in 2004. It is a visual as well as sumptuous treat.

YIELD: 8 SERVINGS

MERINGUE

	whites from 6 large eggs, preferably from cage-free chickens, at room temperature	1 1/2 cups	superfine sugar
1/4 teaspoon	cream of tartar	1 cup	skinned, toasted hazelnuts, finely chopped

Preheat the oven to 325°F.

Coat a 12-by-15-inch baking sheet with non-stick cooking spray and line it with parchment. Lightly spray the parchment.

In the bowl of a stand mixer fitted with the whisk attachment, or in a large stainless steel bowl with a hand held beater, beat the egg whites until they begin to foam. Add the cream of tartar and continue to whip the egg whites at medium speed until they form soft, slightly drooping peaks when the beaters are lifted out.

Turn the speed to high and continue to whip the egg whites as you gradually add the superfine sugar a tablespoon at a time. Beat until the meringue is shiny and holds stiff, upright peaks when the beaters are lifted out. Take care not to over beat. Fold in the chopped hazelnuts.

Scrape the meringue onto the baking sheet and, using an offset spatula, spread it in an even layer over the entire surface of the pan. Place the meringue in the oven on the middle rack and bake for 30 to 35 minutes, or until it is light brown and crisp. Turn off the oven and leave the meringue in it for one hour with the heat off. Remove the meringue from the oven and allow it to cool. When it's completely cooled, remove it from the baking sheet and, using a serrated knife, carefully cut it crosswise into three equal pieces. Set the meringue slices aside on sheets of parchment paper.

GANACHE GLAZE AND FILLING

8 ounces	bittersweet chocolate	2 tablespoons	light corn syrup
1 cup	heavy cream		

Chop the chocolate into 1/4-inch pieces and place in a heat-proof bowl. Bring the cream to a boil in a saucepan or in the microwave and pour it over the chocolate. Gently tap the bowl on your work surface so that the chocolate settles into the cream and allow it to sit for 1 minute.

Using a plastic spatula, stir the mixture, scraping the bottom of the bowl until the chocolate and cream are nicely blended and completely smooth.

(Continued at left)

LAWRY'S RESTAURANT
ENGLISH TRIFLE

This is a beautiful centerpiece dessert that is a favorite of Lawry's. It's even more tempting served in a glass punch bowl.

YIELD: 12 SERVINGS

VANILLA-PUDDING SAUCE

1 package (4.6 ounces)	vanilla pudding mix	2 1/4 cups	whipping cream, divided
2 cups	half-and-half	3 tablespoons	granulated sugar, divided
2 tablespoons	dark rum		

In a medium saucepan combine pudding mix and half-and-half. Cook on moderate heat, stirring continually until the mixture thickens and comes to a boil. Stir in the rum and allow the sauce to cool, then place it in the refrigerator to chill.

Whip half of the whipping cream (1 1/4 cups) and 1 tablespoon of the sugar until the mixture is stiff. Fold this into the chilled pudding.

Whip the remaining 1 1/4 cups of whipping cream with the remaining 2 tablespoons of sugar and place it in the refrigerator to cool. It will be used in the assembly of the trifle.

TO ASSEMBLE

2 tablespoons	red-raspberry preserves	1/4 cup	dry sherry
1	10-inch round layer		strawberries or raspberries
	of sponge cake		the remaining 1 1/4 cups
1/4 cup	brandy		whipped cream

Coat the inside of a 10-inch-deep bowl with the raspberry preserves to within 1 inch of top. Slice the sponge cake horizontally into fourths. Place the top cake slice, crust side up, in the bottom of the bowl, curving edges of cake upward.

In a small bowl combine the brandy and sherry. Sprinkle about 2 tablespoons of this mixture over the cake slice. Spread one third of the chilled vanilla-pudding sauce over the cake slice. Repeat this procedure two more times.

Arrange 15 strawberries or raspberries on top layer of the trifle. Cover with berries with the fourth cake layer, crust side down. Sprinkle the cake with the remaining brandy-sherry mixture.

Place the sweetened whipped cream that had been set aside into a pastry tube fitted with star tip. Pipe 12 small mounds of whipped cream around the edges of the bowl, just below the top, and three more mounds across the diameter. Top each mound with one of the remaining strawberries or raspberries. Chill at least 6 hours before serving.

Recipe courtesy of Ruth Dosti
Dear S.O.S – 30 Years of Recipe Requests to the Los Angeles Times

The Lawry's group now comprises several restaurants in different cities around he country, but the original is in Beverly Hills. And the place is still known around town for its Beef Bowl, in which the teams facing off in the Rose Bowl are treated to a large steak dinner before the game. The finale to the meal is Lawry's English Trifle dessert.

The restaurant showcases this trifle in its glass bowl, so it can be enjoyed visually before each luscious bite of it is eaten.

The original Lawry's opened on La Cienega Boulevard in 1938 and is still owned and operated by the Lawrence L.Frank and Walter Van de Kamp families. Upon visiting the restaurant you'll be greeted with a warm and comfortable home-style environment, and you'll find the service staff most knowledgeable about the restaurant and menu items. Presentation is a very important part of the Lawry's experience, and the entrée is served tableside from a silver cart. You may even be served by one of the Frank or Van de Kamp family members. And you'll find the famous Lawry's seasoned salt at every table.

Among the many awards and recognitions Lawry's has received over the years are the 1999 Legendary Restaurant Award and the 2001 Hall of Fame Award from the Dining Professionals of America. Lawry's was also chosen by The Los Angeles Times Magazine as one of the Top 40 Best Restaurants in Los Angeles for 2001.

Polo Lounge

You don't have to be a star to enjoy this wonderful piece of Hollywood history located in the famous Beverly Hills Hotel. The Polo Lounge evokes the glitter of Tinsel Town at its very best. It is so named because the stars and other notables used to gather there after polo matches.

Each huge, luxurious leather booth allows you to relax with room to spare. In earlier days you could plug in your private telephone so as not to miss some important message. The Polo Lounge is still a watering hole for celebrities and deal makers who want to embrace some of the Hollywood's timeless glamour.

(Continued from right)
In a large mixing bowl, pour the boiled cream over the white chocolate in order to melt it. Allow to cool. Then add the remaining 1 1/3 cups of cream and vanilla and mix until it forms medium peaks. Let this mixture set for 3 hours.

Place mixture in a pastry bag with a round tip and pipe three cone shaped discs on the top of each blondie rectangle.

LEMON-THYME SAUCE

3/4 cup	Water
1 cup	Granulated sugar
	juice of one lemon
	zest of one lemon
	lemon thyme
	lemon sorbet, for garnish

In a small saucepan combine the water and sugar and cook until sugar is dissolved. Allow to cool before adding the lemon juice and lemon thyme. Place in blender and puree.

Place the blondie with the strawberry gelee and white-chocolate topping on a plate. Place a teaspoon of strawberry gelee and lemon thyme sauce on each plate. Add an egg-shaped tablespoon of lemon sorbet aside each blondie and serve.

MACADAMIA BLONDIE
WITH WHITE CHOCOLATE CREAM
AND STRAWBERRY GELÉE

The Polo Lounge, located in the famous Beverly Hills Hotel has been a favorite dining destination for generations of stars and Hollywood deal-makers. This dessert was created to make anyone feel like a star, thanks to executive chef Alex Chen and pastry chef Jean-Francois Suteau. Though it's not easy to prepare. It is well worth the effort.

YIELD: 24 SERVINGS

BLONDIE

8 tablespoons (1 stick)	unsalted butter		1/4 cup	almond paste
1/3 cup	white chocolate, melted		1 cup	all purpose flour, sifted
4 large	eggs		1 1/3 cup	macadamia nuts, chopped
1 1/3 cup	granulated sugar			

Preheat oven to 350°F

In a mixing bowl combine the softened butter with the melted chocolate. In a separate bowl combine the eggs, sugar and almond paste and add them to the butter and chocolate mixture. Add the sifted flour and the macadamia nuts and mix everything well.

Pour the blondie into a 13-by-18-inch baking pan and bake for 20 to 25 minutes. Set aside.

STRAWBERRY GELÉE

6 teaspoons	powered gelatin		1 teaspoon	lemon juice
3/4 cup	water		1 cup	granulated sugar
1	20-ounce package of frozen strawberries or 20 ounces of fresh strawberries			

Add the gelatin to the 3/4 cup of water in a small bowl and allow it to dissolve.

Place the strawberries and sugar in a saucepan over medium heat and cook until the sugar is dissolved. Remove 1/4 cup of the strawberry mixture and set aside for plating. Add the dissolved gelatin to the remaining strawberries in the saucepan and heat until the gelatin is incorporated with the strawberries and sugar. Pour this mixture on top of the blondie and allow it to cool.

Once it has cooled, cut the blondie into rectangles measuring 1 1/2 by 2 1/2 inches.

WHITE CHOCOLATE CREAM

2/3 cup plus 1 tablespoon	heavy cream		3 ounces	white chocolate
1 tablespoon	honey		1 1/3 cups	heavy cream
1 tablespoon	light corn syrup		1 teaspoon	vanilla extract

Place the heavy cream, honey and light corn syrup in a medium saucepan and bring to a boil. Remove from heat. Allow to cool.

(Continued at left)

BANANA SHORTCAKE

Chasen's restaurant on Beverly Boulevard originally focused on hearty American/Continental fare and became especially famous for dishes like chili and hobo steak. For dessert, the banana shortcake was always a crowd-pleaser, and we're pleased to pass along the recipe for this old Hollywood favorite.

YIELD: 6-8 Servings

BANANA SAUCE

1 cup	vanilla ice cream	1 medium	banana, chopped
1/2 cup	heavy cream	1 tablespoon	dark rum, optional

Place the ice cream in a large mixing bowl and set aside to allow the ice cream to soften. In a separate bowl whip the cream until soft peaks form. Add the whipped cream, chopped bananas and optional rum to the ice cream and combine everything well. Set Aside.

CAKE

1 1/2 cups	heavy cream whipped	2 to 3	medium ripe bananas, sliced
3 to 4 tablespoons	granulated sugar		hot fudge sauce, optional
1	baked angel food, sponge or pound cake, about 9 by 5 inches		

In a large mixing bowl whip the cream until soft peaks form. Stir in the sugar to taste.

Slice the cake horizontally into two layers. Place one layer on a serving platter. Spread some of the cream generously over the first cake layer. Peel and slice the bananas and lay them in a single layer over the cream. Spread more cream to cover the bananas. Top with the second cake layer. Frost the top and sides of the cake with the remaining cream. Cover and chill until ready to serve. (The cake may be prepared to this point several hours ahead of serving time.)

To serve, arrange more banana slices over the top of the cake. Slice the cake crosswise into six pieces. Place each cake slice, cut side down, on a plate. Top with the banana sauce and, if desired, hot fudge sauce.

The Great New Rendezvous For Lunch

With a reputation for his culinary skills and with friends in high places, Dave Chasen opened Chasen's Southern Pit in Beverly Hills in 1936. With a policy of keeping photographers and gossip columnists away, the restaurant, with its comfy red-leather booths and wood paneling, eventually became a regular hangout for Hollywood's elite.

The regulars included Clark Gable, Frank Sinatra, Dean Martin, Cary Grant, Alfred Hitchcock and Jimmy Stewart. The stories and lore from the original Chasen's, which closed in 1995, are aplenty.

Former President Ronald Reagan proposed to a then-Nancy Davis at Chasen's, and his regular booth is now enshrined in the Ronald Reagan Presidential Library and Museum in Simi Valley, Calif. Actors Humphrey Bogart and Peter Lorre once got drunk together at the bar and 'stole' the restaurant's hefty safe only to leave it outside on Beverly Boulevard.

Tastes in Hollywood change with the times, and while restaurants like the original Chasen's, Romanoff's or the Brown Derby are no longer serving up their famous dishes, recipes like Chasen's Banana Shortcake live on.

Two of America's most beloved chefs, Mary Sue Milliken and Susan Feniger, own and operate the popular Ciudad Restaurant in downtown Los Angeles. That's where you'll find an upscale, vibrant environment representing the bold, seductive flavors of the Latin World. The service is friendly and the menu is filled with good value and ingenuity.

Mary Sue and Susan have been business partners for more than 25 years, presenting creative, delicious dishes in addition to being extremely prolific in many media outlets. They create homemade desserts such as this Tres Leches Cake with homemade condensed milk. The recipe underwent much testing and trials to produce the silky richness that you'll find here.

Check out Mary Sue and Susan on the Food Network's popular series 'Tamales World Tour' and 'Too Hot Tamales.' Ciudad's creations were also featured in the Samuel Goldwyn feature film 'Tortilla Soup.'

(Continued from right)
When cake is cool, remove it from the pan and trim off the browned top, bottom and side surfaces of the cake. Clean cake pan and line it with two long, criss-crossed pieces of plastic wrap. Return the cake to the pan and slowly pour the tres leches milk mixture over it. Fold the ends of the plastic over the top of the cake to enclose it completely and refrigerate overnight. (The cake should be soaked a day in advance to have lots of time to absorb the milk).

Just before serving, unwrap the cake and turn it upside down onto a 10-inch plate with upturned edges to catch the excess milk. Pipe whipped cream on top of the cake and serve ice cold accompanied by a fruit sauce or two such as passionfruit, mango or raspberry.

CIUDAD
TRES LECHES CAKE

The bold, seductive flavors of Cuba comes out in this Tres Leches cake made with homemade sweetened condensed milk and served with a fruit sauce of your choice (raspberry, mango or passionfruit).

YIELD: 8 SERVINGS

HOME-MADE SWEETENED CONDENSED MILK (MAKES 2 CUPS)

2 cups	nonfat milk	3 tablespoons	granulated sugar
2 cups	whole milk		

Pour the non-fat and whole milks into a medium-heavy saucepan and bring the mixture to a boil. Reduce to a simmer and cook for 4 minutes, stirring occasionally. Stir the sugar into the milk and continue simmering until it is reduced to 2 cups, about 30 – 45 minutes. Strain into a container and refrigerate for as long as one week.

TRES LECHES MILK

2 cups	home-made sweetened condensed milk, chilled	3 cups (2 12-ounce cans)	evaporated milk
2/3 cup	canned sweetened condensed milk	5 ounces	whole milk

Combine all ingredients and reserve in refrigerator.

CAKE

7 large	eggs	2 1/2 cups	cake flour
1 tablespoon	vanilla extract		whipped cream for serving
1 1/2 teaspoon	salt		Fruit sauce for serving
1 1/4 cups	granulated sugar		

Preheat oven to 350°F

Lightly butter and flour a 10" round, 3-inch deep cake pan.

Place the eggs, vanilla, salt and sugar into a large mixer bowl. Place a 5 quart pot half filled with water on medium heat. Place the bowl with the egg mixture on top of the pot (the water in the pot should not reach the bottom of this bowl). Whisk the egg mixture until warm to the touch (100° if using a thermometer). (You must warm the egg mixture before whipping. If not, you will not gain enough air in your sponge cake.) Remove the mixer bowl from this pot and put it on the mixer with whip attachment. Beat the egg mixture at medium speed until it almost doubles in volume, about 10 – 15 minutes.

Meanwhile, sift the flour twice. Remove bowl from the mixer and sift the flour for a third time into the whipped egg mixture while folding very gently yet thoroughly. Pour the finished batter into the prepared cake pan and bake until the cake bounces back when pressed in center, about 40 to 50 minutes. Remove the cake from the oven and allow it to cool completely.
(Continued at left)

Chocolate Coconut Cupcakes

These cupcakes have become a signature of Joan McNamara's culinary skills and the most sought after of her cupcake offerings.

YIELD: 24

CUPCAKES

2/3 cup	chocolate chips	1/2 teaspoon	baking powder
1 cup	boiling water	1/2 teaspoon	salt
2 cups	granulated sugar	2 large	eggs
1 5/8 cups	all-purpose flour	1 cup	buttermilk
1 cup	cocoa powder	1/2 cup	vegetable oil
1 teaspoon	baking soda	1/2 teaspoon	vanilla extract

Preheat the oven to 325°F

Line cupcake pan(s) with paper cups.

Heat the water. Place the chocolate chips in a medium mixing bowl. When the water reaches a boil, pour it over the chips. Let the mixture sit for 5 minutes, then whisk until smooth.

In a large mixing bowl, combine the sugar, flour, cocoa, baking soda, baking powder and salt and whisk until blended.

In a separate medium bowl, combine the eggs, buttermilk, oil and vanilla and whisk to blend. Set this aside.

Add the melted chocolate to the dry ingredients. Using a hand-held mixer with beaters or a stand mixer with the paddle attachment, mix on low speed until everything is combined. Add the egg mixture slowly and beat the batter until smooth.

Pour the batter into the paper cups in the pan.

Bake in the middle of the oven for 20 to 25 minutes, or until the cake springs back to the touch. Cool completely before frosting.

FROSTING

8 ounces)	cream cheese	1/2 teaspoon	vanilla extract
1/3 pound (or 10 1/2 tablespoons)	softened	4 3/4 cups	powdered sugar
	unsalted butter	4 cups	sweet coconut flakes

With the hand-held or stand mixer, beat the butter and cream cheese on the first speed with the paddle attachment or beaters until the ingredients are combined. Add the vanilla and scrape the frosting down the side of the mixing bowl. Add the powdered sugar at once and pulse on first speed until combined, then mix on second speed for about three minutes until light and fluffy.

Place the coconut flakes in a bowl. Spread approximately 2 tablespoons of frosting onto each cupcake and gently roll each onto the coconut flakes to coat the top nicely.

Joan's on Third has become a popular stop among Angelenos when they're searching the culinary landscape for breakfast or lunch. The New York Times Magazine calls it "a magical, soul-nourishing eatery."

The combination shop and restaurant is owned by chef Joan McNamara and her two daughters, Carol and Susie. Joan's is known for its gourmet comfort food. It's also a place where one may spot such celebrities as Jennifer Aniston, Halle Berry or Robert Duvall.

It's a culinary emporium, offering an extensive collection of cheeses, olives and other carefully selected gourmet items from around the world – in addition to its own tempting pastries and food items.

These chocolate coconut cupcakes were cited by McNamara as one of the most popular of the establishment's pastry options. They are super moist, iced in butter cream and abundantly topped with sweet coconut flakes.

When Nancy Silverton was planning to open the Campanile restaurant in Los Angeles, she decided that the hearth-baked bread they wanted to serve in the dining room needed to be baked on-site. Thus began the story of the LaBrea Bakery, which now has its breads and baked goods available in food markets throughout the country. LaBrea has grown to become the largest artisanal bakery in the United States.

The delicacy and elegance of all the LaBrea breads are epitomized in these ginger scones. (When I was test cooking them everything smelled so heavenly that I was taken back to my Grandmother's kitchen, a place where you were almost hugged by the food; the scones are that good.)

The recipe comes to us courtesy of Nancy Silverton, who was cited as Best Pastry Chef of 1991 by the James Beard Foundation.

GINGER SCONES

Here is a traditional cream scone that excites any breakfast with a spicy, ginger surprise in every bite. After all these years, it is still one of the most popular scones sold at the LaBrea Bakery in Los Angeles.

NOTE: You will need a 3-inch round cutter to form the scones.

YIELD: 8 SCONES

2 1/4 cups	unbleached all-purpose flour	2/3 cup	candied ginger, finely chopped into 1/4-inch pieces
1/3 cup	granulated sugar		
1 tablespoon	baking powder	1/2 to 3/4 cup	heavy cream, plus extra for brushing the tops of the scones
1 teaspoon	finely chopped lemon zest (about 1/2 lemon)		
1 1/2 sticks (12 tablespoons)	unsalted butter, cut into 1-inch cubes and frozen		

Adjust the oven rack to the middle position and preheat the oven to 400°F.

In the bowl of a food processor fitted with the steel blade, or in the bowl of an electric mixer fitted with the paddle attachment, combine the flour, sugar, and baking powder. Pulse or mix on low to incorporate. Add the lemon zest and butter, and pulse on and off or mix on low, until the mixture is pale yellow and the consistency of a fine meal.

Transfer the mixture to a large bowl and stir in the ginger. Make a well in the center and pour in 1/2 cup of the cream. Using one hand, draw in the dry ingredients, mixing until just combined. If the mixture feels dry, add the remaining 1/4 cup of the cream.

Wash and dry your hands and dust them with flour. Turn the dough out onto a lightly floured work surface and gently knead a few times to gather into a ball. Roll or pat the dough into a circle about 3/4-inch thick. Cut out the circles, cutting as closely together as possible and keeping the trimming intact.

Gather the scraps, pat and press the pieces back together, and cut out the remaining dough. Place the scones 1 inch apart on a parchment-lined baking sheet.

Brush the tops with the remaining cream.

Bake for 12 to 16 minutes, or until the surface cracks and they are slightly browned.

Tres Leches Berry Trifle

As you'll see in the list of ingredients, 'Tres Leches' translates as 'three milks.'

One of the restaurant chef's greatest challenges is to come up with new twists to customers' favorite desserts. This cake by Porto's Chef Tony Salazar is a favorite of his fans, and it remains true to its Cuban heritage. Changing the presentation slightly by placing the cake in a glass or a single serving cup and adding fresh seasonal berries, Salazar makes it a treat for the eyes as well as for the taste buds.

YIELD: 12 SERVINGS

CAKE

6 large	eggs, separated	3 tablespoons	whole milk
1/4 cup	granulated sugar, divided	1/4 teaspoon	vanilla
3/4 cup	cake flour		

Preheat the oven to 350°F.

Sift the cake flour and set it aside. Grease and flour either one 12-by-15-inch sheet pan or two 8-inch round cake pans lined with parchment or wax paper.

Prepare the cake batter by first separating the eggs, placing the yolks in one large mixing bowl and the whites in another.

Add 1/8 cup (2 tablespoons) of the sugar to the yolks and beat the mixture to the ribbon stage (reached when a spoon dipped into the mixture leaves a trail behind that is visible for a short while) about 3 to 5 minutes. The mixture should be pale yellow. Add and stir the sifted cake flour and milk into the yolk mixture in three stages. That is, add 1/4 cup of cake flour and 1 to 2 tablespoons of whole milk at a time, being careful not to deflate the mixture.

In the other mixing bowl with the egg whites, combine them with 1/8 cup (two tablespoons) of sugar. With an electric mixer, whip on medium speed to a soft-peak stage. The mixture will be shiny.

Add 1/3 of the egg whites and sugar to the yolk mixture and fold in the whites carefully so as not to deflate the mixture. Add the remaining 2/3 of the egg whites and sugar and carefully fold them in until everything is blended well. The mixture should be smooth and fluffy, not runny. Carefully spread the batter evenly into the prepared pan(s) and bake the cake for 8 to 10 minutes until light golden brown.

MILK/CREAM FILLING FOR CAKE

1 can (12 ounces)	evaporated milk	3/4 cup	heavy cream
1 can (14 ounces)	sweetened condensed milk		

In medium-size bowl, mix the evaporated and condensed milks and cream until blended.

Remove the cake from the pan and flip it over by placing another piece of paper on top of it. Gently pierce the cake with a table fork every few inches and pour the milk-and-cream filling onto the cake, allowing the filling to penetrate the cake. Let this rest for 10 to 15 minutes to allow the cake to absorb the liquid.

(Continued at right)

Porto's Bakery is one of the oldest Cuban bakeries in the Los Angeles area. It began as a cottage industry in Cuba when Rosa Porto, after losing her job, began baking and selling cakes and pies to pay the bills. In 1971 she and husband Raul moved to Los Angeles where she continued her home baking business. Demand soon outgrew her kitchen capacity, and today there are two Porto's Bakery locations, along with another facility for production.

Current Executive Chef Tony Salazar also moved to Los Angeles from Cuba, and became fast friends with the Porto's son, Raul Jr. Salazar even spent time helping out his friend at the family bakery after school. Following formal culinary training, and working his way up at Porto's, Tony eventually took over the executive chef reigns. Raul Jr. is now the president.

Chef Tony offers this twist on the traditional Tres Leches Cake by serving it in a glass cup and adding fresh fruit and berries (a trifle). It's a prime example of a classic dessert with a new soul that's become part of the Porto's identity.

(Continued from left)

WHIPPED CREAM

2 cups	heavy whipping cream
1 tablespoon	granulated sugar
1/4 cup	brandy or rum, optional
4 pints	seasonal berries or fruits

In a medium, chilled metal bowl, whip the cream until soft peaks form. Add the sugar (and brandy or rum if desired) and continue whipping until no grittiness remains. In a glass dessert cup or drinking glasses, place a layer of the cake at the bottom, followed by a layer of whipped cream, place berries on top of this and continue with another layer of cake, whipped cream and finished with fruit on top.

Proprietor-chef Suzanne Goin named her restaurant Lucques after her favorite Languedoc French olive, one that is highly prized by gourmets. It was only a matter of time before the restaurant itself became highly valued by its clientele.

Committed to serving only the freshest ingredients in novel and flawless ways, Goin draws on her experiences with great chefs and restaurants in the United States and France. Among them are Alice Waters of Chez Panisse, Todd English of Olives and Alain Passard of Arpege.

Suzanne works closely with local and organic farmers to acquire the best products for her dishes, which are presented with a combination of chic and rusticity. Reading this recipe for a crème fraiche panna cotta one can almost taste the California sunshine in the fresh blackberries, which are combined with cinnamon and crème de cassis, and warmed with peppercorns and thyme. It is truly a delightful and original dessert.

Goin was named Best Chef in California by the James Beard Foundation in 2006. Her cookbook "Sunday Suppers at Lucques" was recently published.

LUCQUES

Crème Fraîche Panna Cotta
with Blackberry Compote

This is a dessert that looks as georgeous as it tastes when served in pretty glasses topped with this rich blackberry compote and presented with French butter cookies. (page 74) It comes to us compliments of pastry chef Breanne Varela.

YIELD: 8 SERVINGS

PANNA COTTA

3 cups	heavy cream		5 tablespoons	granulated sugar
1/2 cup	whole milk		1/2 cup plus 2 tablespoons	crème fraîche*
4 teaspoons	Knox gelatin powder			

Sour cream may be used in place of the crème fraîche.

Pour the cream and milk into a 2-quart saucepan and sprinkle the gelatin powder over the surface. Allow 5 to 10 minutes for the powder to dissolve. After it is dissolved, stir the mixture gently. Stir in the sugar and place the mixture on medium-high heat. When small bubbles begin to form around the edge of the saucepan, the panna cotta is ready. Remove it from heat, whisk it well, and allow to cool. When it has cooled, slowly whisk in the crème fraîche. Pour the panna cotta evenly into eight 4-ounce serving glasses or ramekins and place them in the refrigerator for 4 to 8 hours to set.

BLACKBERRY COMPOTE

1	5"x5" piece of cheesecloth		1/4 cup	water
1/2	vanilla bean pod, with scraped seeds		1/2 cup	granulated sugar
			1/4 cup	crème de cassis liquor
1/2	cinnamon stick		2 pints	whole blackberries, divided
1/4 teaspoon	black peppercorns		1/4 teaspoon	thyme leaves

Create a sachet by first placing the cheesecloth on a work surface. Place the vanilla bean pod and its seeds, cinnamon stick and black peppercorns in the center of the cheesecloth. Bring the corners of the cheesecloth to the center and tie them together with a piece of butcher's twine to form the sachet. Set it aside.

Pour the water into a 1 quart, non-reactive saucepan. Add the sugar and place the saucepan on medium-high heat. When the sugar begins to caramelize, carefully swirl the sugar around to ensure an even caramel. When the caramel reaches the color of peanut butter, turn off the heat. Slowly and carefully pour in the crème de cassis liqueur. This will produce considerable steam, so be careful. When the steam subsides, add the sachet of spices and 1 pint of the blackberries. Reduce the heat to low and cook 15 minutes.

When the cooking is done, remove the sachet with a spoon. Strain the remaining mixture through the finest strainer available and toss it with the remaining 1 pint of blackberries and the thyme leaves. Place the compote in the refrigerator for about 1 hour to cool.

At serving time, if using glasses, place each glass on a serving plate. If using ramekins, set them into a pan of hot water for a few seconds, then reverse the panna cottas onto the plates. Spoon about 1 tablespoon of blackberry compote on top of each. Place two French butter cookies beside each serving.

White Coffee Crème Brûlée

Chateau Marmont
hollywood

Here is a lusty example of having your after dinner coffee and dessert too. Chef Carolynn Spence captures the sweetness of crème brûlée and infuses it with espresso beans.

YIELD: 6 SERVINGS

4 cups	heavy cream	12 large	egg yolks
1 cup	whole milk	3/4 cup	granulated sugar
1/2 cup	espresso coffee beans		Additional sugar for
1/2	vanilla bean, scraped		dusting the custards

Preheat the oven to 300°F.

Pour the heavy cream and milk into a medium saucepan. Add the coffee and vanilla pod and seeds and cook over low heat for 20 minutes to allow the coffee and vanilla to infuse the cream and milk. Turn off heat and let the mixture sit for 10 minutes.

In a separate bowl, whisk together the egg yolks and sugar. With a ladle, slowly stir in the warm cream mixture to the egg yolks and sugar until everything is completely combined. Strain the custard into a separate bowl and allow it to cool.

Place six 6-ounce molds or cups into a deep baking pan. (The kitchen at the Chateau Marmont uses coffee cups.)

Pour some of the custard base into each mold or cup. Fill the pan with warm water to immerse the molds or cups 3/4 of the way up the rims.

Cover the custards with a sheet of aluminum foil and bake, about 45 minutes or until the custards are set and the centers jiggle slightly.

Allow the custards to cool, then refrigerate them until needed.

At serving time, dust the top of each cold custard evenly with sugar. Using either a torch or the oven broiler on high, caramelize the sugar as evenly as possible.

Garnish the crème brûlées with berries, chocolate-covered espresso beans or cookies.

Chateau Marmont is the perfect reflection of the glitter of Los Angeles. This fabled hotel, restaurant and bar located on a hill near the famous Sunset Strip holds a treasure trove of stories featuring the legendary actors and rock stars who have populated Hollywood over the years.

Built in 1927, and modeled after a French Chateau, it sports multiple period rooms, cottages and bungalows, and always has been known for the notable people and events it has served over its 80-year history. If walls could talk, they would tell of James Dean hopping in through a window to audition with Natalie Wood and Sal Mineo for 'Rebel Without a Cause,' or the Led Zeppelin band members riding their motorcycles through the hotel lobby.

The beautiful garden serves meals throughout the year, and the ambience of the Marmont's flora, fauna and Gothic architecture can be enjoyed in seclusion from the noise of the Sunset Strip.

The addition of Carolynn Spence, former chef de cuisine at the Spotted Pig in New York, to the restaurant's culinary staff has added creative presentations to this class act. Her White Coffee Crème Brûlée is a dreamy example of her bold, yet simple flavors designed for those who love dessert.

When I first stepped into Palate it was mid-afternoon, long past lunch, and we wanted to taste the new food, sample the wine and try a dessert. We expected the food to be special since the chef-owner Octavio Becerra had formerly partnered with Joachim Splichal and the Patina Group before starting out on his own with Palate.

The food was exceptional. The Porkfolio plate was just right with selections of prosciutto, salumi and bresaola. The recommended wine was delightful and the only dessert available at that time was the chocolate pudding. I would have been seduced by the chocolate pudding alone. It was wonderful.

Located in a former moving and storage warehouse with high ceilings and a walk-in cheese humidor, Palate offers a surprise at every step. It's a wine bar, a culinary library and a wine shop, and you must walk through the entire space in order to find all its offerings. Partner Steve Goldrun is the wine guru and pairs the simple, down-to-earth food with complementing wines.

Enjoy small plates of Dungeness crab, squash blossom salad and chicken liver crostini.

Cheeses as well as charcuterie and local and artisanal ingredients are a few of the elements that set this culinary experience apart from others.

CHOCOLATE PUDDING

This is rich and luscious chocolate crème pudding. It's served with a dollop of crème fraîche and spoonful of chopped, macerated strawberries on top. A very smooth finale to any of Palate's entrees.

YIELD: 8 SERVINGS

1/2 cup	medium-chopped strawberries	1/4 cup, plus 2 tablespoons	cocoa powder
1 teaspoon	granulated sugar	1/4 cup	cornstarch
1 1/2 ounces	bittersweet chocolate, preferably Valrhona, finely chopped	Pinch	kosher salt
		2 cups	milk
		1 cup	half and half
1 1/2 ounces	white chocolate, finely chopped	1 1/2 teaspoons	vanilla extract
3/4 cups	granulated sugar	1 cup	whipped crème fraîche or whipped cream, for garnish

In a small bowl, combine the chopped strawberries with the granulated sugar. Set aside.

In a large mixing bowl, combine the bittersweet and white chocolates. Set aside.

In a medium mixing bowl, whisk together the sugar, cocoa powder, cornstarch and salt. Slowly add the milk, then the half-and-half, whisking until smooth.

Pour the mixture through a fine sieve unto a medium, heavy-bottom saucepan. Bring the mixture to a boil over medium heat, whisking continuously. This will activate the cornstarch to thicken the pudding. To prevent burning, be sure to reach all sides and the bottom of the pan while constantly whisking so the ingredients do not settle. Reduce the heat to a gentle simmer and cook an additional 2 minutes, whisking continuously. Immediately remove from heat and whisk in the vanilla extract. Strain the mixture into the bowl with the chocolate, stirring to melt the chocolate, and incorporate it into the pudding. Place the bowl over an ice bath and continue to stir until the mixture cools, stirring occasionally.

Divide the mixture between eight 3-ounce ramekins or similarly small sized small coffee cups or sherbet glasses. Refrigerate the puddings until well chilled. To prevent a 'skin' from forming on top of the puddings, place a small sheet of plastic wrap directly on the surface of each pudding.

Serve the puddings topped with mascerated strawberries and a little whipped crème fraîche or cream.

BUTTERSCOTCH BUDINO
WITH CARAMEL SAUCE

This attention-getting dessert is not too sweet, and titillates the taste buds with a sprinkle of Maldon sea salt or fleur de sel on the caramel topping. The budino delivers a little surprise with each spoonful. It comes to us from Mozza's co-owners and chefs Nancy Silverton, Mario Batali and Joseph Bastianich along with executive pastry chef Dahlia Narvaez.

SERVES: 10

BUDINO

3 cups	heavy cream	1/2 cup	water	
1 1/2 cups	whole milk	1 1/8 cups	dark brown sugar	
1 large	egg	1 1/2 teaspoons	kosher salt	
3 large	egg yolks	5 tablespoons	unsalted butter	
5 tablespoons	cornstarch	1 1/2 tablespoons	dark rum	

In a large bowl, combine the cream and milk and set aside.

In a large, heavy pot, combine the brown sugar, water and salt and place over medium-high heat. Bring the mixture to a boil and cook 10 to 12 minutes, stirring occasionally to keep it from scorching. When it is a deep brown color and smells nutty and caramelized, remove it from heat. Immediately whisk the cream-and-milk mixture into the caramelized sugar to stop the cooking. The caramel cream will steam vigorously and the sugar will seize. Use caution to keep from getting burned by the bubbling mixture. Whisk until the caramel cream is fully incorporated and the mixture is smooth. Return to high heat. When it reaches a boil, turn off the heat.

In a bowl, whisk together the egg, egg yolks and cornstarch. While whisking constantly, add about half of the caramel cream, 1/2 cup at a time, to the egg mixture. Keep the remaining caramel cream in the saucepan.

Pour the combined mixtures back into the saucepan holding the remaining caramel cream. Cook over medium heat, whisking constantly, for about 2 minutes, or until a very thick custard forms.

Remove the custard from heat and whisk in the butter and rum. Pour the custard through a fine-mesh strainer or sieve into ten 3/4-cup ramekins or glasses, dividing it evenly and filling each to within 1/2 inch of the rim. Cover with plastic wrap and refrigerate for at least 2 hours, or until well chilled, or for up to 3 days.

SAUCE AND TOPPING

3/4 cup	heavy cream	2 tablespoons	light corn syrup
1	1-inch piece of vanilla bean or 1/4 teaspoon of vanilla extract	1/2 cup	granulated sugar
		3 to 4 tablespoons	water
		3/4 cup	crème fraîche
2 tablespoons	unsalted butter	1 1/4 teaspoon	Maldon sea salt or fleur de sel

(Continued at right)

(Continued from left)

Place 1/2 cup of the cream and the vanilla bean in a medium saucepan. Heat until simmering. Add the butter to the cream and vanilla, stir, and remove the mixture from heat. Set aside.

In a large, heavy-bottomed saucepan, combine the corn syrup, sugar and enough water (3 to 4 tablespoons) to make a wet, sandy mixture. Cook the mixture over medium-high heat, about 10 minutes, swirling it in the saucepan for even cooking. After about 10 minutes, or when the mixture is a medium amber color, remove it from heat and carefully whisk in the cream and vanilla. Set the mixture aside and allow it to cool. (This may be refrigerated and reheated before serving.)

To make the topping, whisk the remaining 1/4 cup of cream in a large bowl until it begins to thicken. Add the crème fraîche and whisk until thick and fluffy.

To serve, spoon a tablespoon of warm caramel sauce over each budino. Sprinkle each with 1/8 teaspoon of Maldon sea salt or fleur de sel and top with a dollop of the heavy-cream-and-crème-fraîche mixture.

Founded in 1927 by George and Aurelia Salisbury, El Cholo is Los Angeles' oldest Mexican restaurant. El Cholo, a name which was given to field workers by early Spanish settlers in California, was written on a napkin with a cartoon doodle and left in the restaurant. This serves as the logo for the restaurant today.

The original El Cholo was located in a small old California bungalow with just eight stools and three booths. It quickly expanded to the rambling restaurant that it is today with new locations in Santa Monica and Pasadena.

Famous stars have enjoyed dining here, among them Gary Cooper, Bing Crosby, Loretta Young, Jack Nicholson, Madonna and Tom Hanks.

Five generations of family members have served the restaurant's famous margaritas, green-corn tamales and vegetarian fajitas. A milestone year for El Cholo was 1996, during which the restaurant is said to have served its 1 billionth tortilla. El Cholo is the world's largest user of Cuervo 1800 premium Tequila. This is also where nachos were introduced to the United States in the 1950's.

EL CHOLO

Flan

Flan is a typical Spanish dessert designed to complement the meal and soothe the palate.

YIELD: 8 SERVINGS

3 large	eggs	1/2 teaspoon	vanilla extract
1 can (14 ounces)	sweetened condensed milk	1/2 cup	granulated sugar
1 cup	whole milk		water

Break the eggs in a small bowl. Place them in a blender container with the condensed milk, whole milk and vanilla extract. Blend thoroughly. (You may also place everything in a large mixing bowl and beat the mixture vigorously with a wire whisk to blend everything well.) Set the mixture aside.

In a heavy skillet over low heat, melt the sugar, stirring occasionally to keep the caramel from scorching. Add a few drops of water a little at a time, stirring until the caramel reaches spreading consistency.

Preheat oven to 350°F.

With a small spoon, distribute the caramel among eight 4-to5-ounce custard cups (or ramekins), tilting the cups to spread the caramel evenly. An option would be to spread the caramel in to a 8-by-8-inch square baking pan with a sufficiently deep rim.

Pour the flan into the caramel-lined cups or the 8-by-8-inch pan. Pour 1/4 inch of hot water into a separate, shallow baking pan. Place the cups (or the pan holding the flans) in the water. Cover the outer pan with foil. If using cups or ramekins, bake for 50 minutes. If using a 8-by-8-inch pan, bake for 1 hour or until firm. Remove the flan(s) from the oven, and, when cool, place them in the refrigerator for about 1 hour to chill slightly.

To serve, first run a sharp knife around the outer edge of the cups or pan. Then invert the flan(s) onto individual small plates or a serving platter. This dessert can be enhanced with such toppings as dollops of whipped cream or a spoonful of chopped fresh fruit.

RED VELVET PUDDING

This is a heavenly dessert that offers a new twist to the classic red velvet cake by de-constructing the cake into a pudding and adding a rich, chocolate-truffle surprise in the center.

The recipe has been modified for home cooking.

YIELD: 16 SERVINGS

RED VELVET CAKE

3 1/2 cups	all purpose flour	1 1/4 cups	vegetable oil
1 1/2 cups	granulated sugar	1 cup	buttermilk
1 teaspoon	baking soda	2 large	eggs
1 teaspoon	cocoa powder	1 teaspoon	white vinegar
1 teaspoon	salt	5 ounces	red food coloring

Preheat oven to 325°F

Combine the flour, sugar, baking soda, cocoa powder and salt in an electric mixer.

Add the oil, buttermilk, eggs, vinegar and coloring to the flour-and-sugar mixture and mix on medium speed until blended.

Pour the batter into baking pans and bake for approximately 30 to 35 minutes, until a toothpick inserted in the center comes out clean. Cool the cake and crumble it into small pieces.

CHOCOLATE PUDDING

1 cup	heavy cream	1/4 cup	granulated sugar
2 ounces	milk	1 ounce	dark chocolate
2 large	egg yolks		

In a medium saucepan, combine cream and milk and bring the mixture to a boil. In a small bowl, whisk the milk and egg yolks until blend and add this mixture to the cream and milk cooking very slowly to keep from cooking the eggs. Pour this warm mixture over the chocolate and let cool.

GANACHE FILLING

8 ounces	dark chocolate	11 ounces	heavy cream

Place the chocolate and cream in a medium, microwave-safe bowl. Heat in the microwave on high power until the mixture is warm to the touch, about 30 seconds. Whisk the mixture until it is smooth, and then chill it.

ASSEMBLY AND BAKING

Preheat oven to 325°F

In a large bowl, combine the crumbled red velvet cake and the chocolate pudding and stir to combine.

(Continued at right)

(Continued from left)

Place 1 ounce (about 2 tablespoons) of this red velvet pudding mixture into 16 buttered, 4 ounce ramekins. Using a 3/4-to-1-inch melon baller, place one ball of ganache in the center of the pudding mixture. Place another 2 tablespoons of the red velvet pudding mixture on top of the ganache and push it down with a spoon so the ganache is completely covered. The ramekin should be completely filled. Flatten or smooth the top as necessary. Bake for 20 minutes. Allow the pudding cake to cool. Then warm it before serving.

RASPBERRY SAUCE

1 basket	raspberries
1/4 cup	granulated sugar
	juice of one lemon

In a small saucepan, combine the raspberries and sugar and bring to a simmer, stirring occasionally. Remove the mixture from heat and stir in the lemon juice. Strain and cool.

PLATING

2 baskets	raspberries 64 to garnish each serving with 4 raspberries mascarpone or vanilla ice cream raspberry sorbet

For each serving, spoon one tablespoon of chocolate sauce (page 90) on a round plate and one tablespoon of raspberry sauce in a circle on the plate. Place the warmed pudding cake in the center of the plate on top of the chocolate sauce. Place two raspberries at the 3 o'clock position on the plate and one raspberry on each side of the pudding cake (4 raspberries total). Place a small spoonful of mascarpone or vanilla ice cream on top of the pudding cake and one small spoonful of raspberry sorbet alongside the raspberries in the 3 o'clock position.

After graduating from the University of California at Berkeley and observing the birthplace of California cuisine at Chez Panisse, Mariah decided that her future would be in the culinary field, and she trained at Le Cordon Bleu College of Culinary Arts in Pasadena. "I had a nasty habit of watching cooking shows on public television while working on my senior thesis. My favorite shows were Baking with Julia and Dessert Circus with Jacques Torres."

She affirms her love of promoting classic dessert preparations using such authentic ingredients as Medjool dates, Empire Apples, treacle, Lyle's golden Syrup and Majarajah curry. Mariah is an energetic force in the kitchen giving us 'just perfect' desserts every time.

Examples of her work can be found at Grace Restaurant and BLD.

MARIAH SWAN

Sticky Toffee Pudding with Toffee Sauce

"We stay true to this classic English dessert by using treacle and Golden syrup in our recipe" says Los Angeles pastry chef Mariah Swan. "While most recipes call for chopped dates, we puree plump, moist Medjool dates before adding them to our batter adding texture and complexity to the pudding." Serve the pudding with a generous helping of toffee sauce, a scoop of hazelnut gelato or vanilla ice cream and sliced, bruleed bananas, for which the recipe is given below.

Note: Golden syrup and treacle can be found at high-end grocery stores and Irish import shops. Dates need to be as large and moist as possible. Dry, hard dates will affect the quality of the batter.

YIELD: 8 SERVINGS

PUDDING

4 1/2 ounces	unsalted butter	2 cups	self-rising flour
2 cups	raw sugar	4 1/2 teaspoons	baking soda
1/3 cup	treacle or molasses	10 ounces	pitted dates, preferably Medjool
3 ounces	golden syrup (corn syrup)	1 1/8 teaspoon	vanilla extract
5 large	eggs		

Preheat oven to 325°F

Grease a 9-inch cake pan and line the bottom of the pan with parchment paper. Grease the parchment paper.

In a large mixing bowl cream together the butter and raw sugar. Add the treacle or molasses and golden syrup and combine them. Scrape the sides of the bowl.

Add the eggs, one at a time, mixing until each is just combined before adding the next egg.

Add the self-rising flour and baking soda and mix to combine. Scrape the bowl.

Puree the dates, hot water and vanilla together. Add this mixture to the batter and mix until just combined.

Pour into batter into the prepared pan and bake until deep brown and center is set, about 45 minutes to 1 hour.

TOFFEE SAUCE

1 cup	granulated sugar	1 1/2 cups	heavy cream, divided
4 tablespoons (1/2 stick)	unsalted butter, divided		salt to taste

In a medium size saucepan cook the sugar, the butter and half of the cream until carmelized and thick, whisking frequently.

Carefully whisk in the remaining cream and cook until emulsified. Add salt to taste.

(Continued at left)

(Continued from right)

BRÛLÉED BANANAS

2 to 3	ripe but firm bananas
2 to 3 tablespoons	granulated sugar

Slice the bananas on an extreme bias into pieces 1/2 inch thick. Sprinkle one side of the banana slices with sugar. Caramelize the sugar with a kitchen torch or place the bananas under a hot broiler to brown the sugar. The torch method is recommended as it doesn't cook the banana, it just caramelizes the sugar.

Panna Cotta
with Rose Petals

"This is my Grandmother's recipe from Sorrento, Italy," says Il Cielo's owner and chef, Pasquale Vericella. "My family loved it for dessert and I knew that I wanted to include it in my restaurant in Beverly Hills." She could have added that the panna cotta's smooth, creamy texture is highlighted by sugared rose petals in any of their seasonal colors.

YIELD: 10 SERVINGS

PANNA COTTA

4 cups	heavy cream	1	Vanilla bean , scraped and seeded
1/4 cup	whipping cream	2 teaspoons	vanilla extract
2/3 cups	granulated sugar	4 teaspoons	powdered gelatin

Combine the heavy cream, whipping cream, sugar and vanilla bean and seeds in a saucepan. Then add the powdered gelatin allowing 2 or 3 minutes for it to dissolve. Simmer until the gelatin has completely dissolved. Let cool to room temperature. Pour the mixture into molds and refrigerate for 4 hours.

SUGARED ROSE PETALS

1 large	egg white	1 cup	superfine (caster) sugar
1 tablespoon	water	24	rose petals

In a small bowl, mix egg white and water until blended. Dip one rose petal at a time in the mixture to coat completely. (Using tweezers or chop sticks works well for the dipping.) Line a baking sheet with parchment paper and then sprinkle both sides of the petal with the sugar and place on the parchment to dry. Let them dry overnight. These may be stored in an airtight container for several months.

RASPBERRY SAUCE

1 pint	raspberries, fresh or frozen	1 tablespoon	lemon juice
1/4 cup	granulated sugar		

In a small saucepan, cook the raspberries with the sugar and lemon juice until the berries release a syrup and the fruit cooks down. Strain the syrup into a small bowl and allow to cool.

TO SERVE

Remove the Panna Cotta by placing each filled ramekin or mold in a bowl of hot water for 5 to 10 seconds, allowing the contents to be released. Then place the serving plate over the top of the ramekin and flip it over onto the plate. Garnish each panna cotta with 4 rose petals and a drizzle of raspberry sauce and 1 or 2 fresh raspberries.

This landmark bungalow-turned-restaurant is nestled in Beverly Hills, one of the most beautiful settings in Los Angeles.

When you step through the vine-covered wrought iron gates you're surrounded by a lush, charming courtyard with a garden. You can dine al fresco or move inside the former home into one of the private dining areas which are reminiscent of the chef-owner's Tuscan roots, with its antique Italian tile floors and stone walls.

Chef Pasquale Vericella searched for years before finding this private residence, that he transformed into the romantic restaurant he wanted to create.

The food is classic Northern Italian and Pasquale credits his mother and grandmother for instilling him with a love of cooking. A couple of favorites are the fava bean soup with fennel and the shrimp with marinated artichoke salad.

Though Il Cielo (the sky) is elegant, it is also comfortable and homey. The surroundings work their magic. The New York Times has cited this as one of the top five places in the United States for weddings, and Il Cielo has hosted hundreds of them.

Loteria Grill, named after a children's game of bingo, first opened in a stall the Farmers Market in Hollywood serving authentic Mexican foods. It continues to be a favorite of many Angelenos.

The market location became so popular that a second location on Hollywood Boulevard was established. There, one can watch the food being cooked while waiting for the order. The open outdoor eating is classic California style.

Using only top quality ingredients, owner and chef Jimmy Shaw offers a mashed potato soft taco, mushroom, and zucchini-succotash tacos for the vegetarian enthusiasts. This is in addition to the slow-roasted pork and the traditional pozole (pork and hominy stew). The tortilla dough is prepared fresh daily.

Try the watermelon-juice drink, and of course, finish with delicious Flan de Cajeta to complete this experience.

LOTERIA GRILL

FLAN DE CAJETA

This is a delicious, silky flan that's easy to make and will win your friends over. Jimmy Shaw has served this flan since his opening of the original Loteria Grill in the original Farmers Market on Fairfax. It has been a "come back to" dessert for many years. The addition of orange juice and Cajeta *(a Mexican caramel made with goat's milk)* give the flan a most delicious flavor. *(Cajeta is available at specialty markets and some supermarkets.)* The flan(s) can be baked either in individual serving containers or in a single glass baking dish.

YIELD: 8 SERVINGS

CARAMEL

1/2 cup	water		3 tablespoons	orange juice
1/2 cup	granulated sugar			

Place the water, sugar and orange juice in a saucepan and cook over low heat, stirring constantly. When the mixture reaches a golden caramel color, remove from heat. After the caramel cools slightly, use it immediately to coat either individual containers, such as ramekins, or an 8-by-8-inch glass baking dish.

FLAN

1 can (12 ounces)	evaporated milk		3 large	eggs
1 can (14 ounces)	sweetened condensed milk		4 tablespoons	cajeta

Preheat oven to 375°F.

Place all ingredients in a blended and mix until smooth. Pour the mixture into the ramekins or a glass baking dish which has been set into a shallow baking pan filled with 1/2 inch of water. Bake for 30-45 minutes, or until a clean toothpick inserted in to the flan(s) come out clean.

Allow the flan(s) to cool at room temperature for approximately 1 hour. Either serve immediately or refrigerate until chilled.

To serve, run a butter knife or small spatula along the edge of the flan and then turn over to release the flan onto the plate, making sure to pour all of the caramel on the flan.

Enjoy with people you love.

Chocolate Chunk Bread Pudding

Here is a simple, sweet, crowd-pleasing dessert – a bread pudding that is easy to make and a favorite of Angeli's customers.

YIELD: 12 SERVINGS

5 large	eggs	1 1/2 cups	heavy cream
4 large	egg yolks	1 loaf	egg bread, crusts removed
1 cup	granulated sugar		and cut into 1/2-inch cubes
1/2 teaspoon	vanilla extract	12 ounces	bittersweet chocolate
5 cups	whole milk		

Preheat oven to 375°F.

In a large mixing bowl, beat the whole eggs, the yolks and the sugar. Add the vanilla, milk, and cream and mix well.

Place the bread cubes into the bowl with the eggs, sugar, milk and cream. Mix well and let the bread begin to absorb the liquid.

Cut the chocolate into roughly 1/2-inch chunks.

Place one half of the soaked bread in a buttered 9-by-13-inch baking dish. Scatter the chocolate chunks amongst the bread. Top with remaining soaked bread. Let everything soak in the refrigerator for up to 24 hours or bake immediately.

Cover baking dish with foil and place it in the oven. Cook until the pudding puffs up and a knife inserted in the middle of the pudding comes out clean, about 1 hour and 30 minutes. Remove the foil and allow the pudding to remain in the oven until it browns just a bit.

Serve warm with whipped cream or ice cream.

Evan Kleiman, the owner of the trattoria named Angeli Caffe, is a chef, a caterer, speaker, writer, radio show host and founder of the Los Angeles chapter of Slow Food, the worldwide organization dedicated to preserving food quality and sustainability. A tomato named for Evan can be found at the Farmers' Market. It's grown from a seed Evan brought back from Italy, and sold by a farmer she persuaded to cultivate the variety.

When not busy at her restaurant or giving inspirational talks, Evan offers gastronomic tours of Italy. That she still finds time to manage a business and produce such imaginative Italian dishes is amazing.

Learning to cook at her mother's side and later spending much time in Italy, Evan learned the basic methods of cooking light, rustic food that can be enjoyed every day. We were delighted with the simple lentil and escarole soup we had at Angeli Caffe, as well as a light salad of farm-fresh peaches and tomatoes. And, yes, we had some time and room for this rich chocolate chunk bread pudding.

The owners of Musso and Frank Grill claim that it's the oldest restaurant in Hollywood, and when you open the door and step inside, you believe it. This is a real time-machine. Leaving the noisy sidewalk and walking into the restaurant transports you to the past. The classically aged wood-paneled walls, the patina of worn leather booths, and the waiters help to conjure up the feeling of living at a slower pace, while enjoying the rich, hearty aromas from the wood-burning grill and the buzz of dining room conversation.

Here you can soak up some Hollywood atmosphere while enjoying such dishes as he famous chicken pot pit (a Wednesday dinner special) and the old fashioned corned beef and cabbage. If you're lucky enough to be served by Manny Aquirre, he just might share stories of the scores of movie legends he's gotten to know about. Afterwards, he'll probably continue to entertain you with the hand tricks he's collected during his many years at Musso and Frank. While you're there, ask Manny to whip up what many consider the best martini in Hollywood.

Among those who've frequented this venue are writers William Faulkner, F. Scott Fitzgerald and Ernest Hemingway and movie stars such as Charlie Chaplin and Raymond Burr.

This diplomat pudding, though very simple, has a long history as a French dessert. Here it's dressed up with macerated strawberries.

MUSSO & FRANK GRILL

DIPLOMAT PUDDING

Musso and Frank, Hollywood's oldest surviving restaurant, has served this old-fashioned pudding to many movie celebrities as well as ordinary folk just hankering for a trip down memory lane.

NOTE: You will need six baking cups, each holding 7 ounces.

YIELD: 6 SERVINGS

4 large	eggs	6 tablespoons	raisins
1/2 cup	granulated sugar	2 tablespoons	butter
3 cups	whole milk	1/2 cup	heavy cream, whipped to
1/2 teaspoon	vanilla extract		soft peaks, optional
3 slices	white bread, cubed		

Preheat oven to 350°F.

In a large mixing bowl beat the eggs and sugar until the mixture is light and creamy. Continue beating, adding the milk and vanilla.

In each of six 7 ounce baking cups, place some of the bread cubes, 1 tablespoon of the raisins and 1 teaspoon of the butter. Add the beaten egg-and-milk mixture until each cup is 2/3 full.

Place the filled cups in baking pan on middle rack of the oven. Pour boiling water into the baking pan half-way up the sides of cups.

Bake until the pudding is set or until a clean knife inserted near center comes out clean, about 25 to 30 minutes. Invert each pudding onto serving plate. Serve with the whipped cream or this strawberry sauce.

STRAWBERRY SAUCE

1 pint	fresh strawberries	2 tablespoons	water
1/2 cup	sugar		

Wash the strawberries well, remove the stems and slice or chop them into a mixing bowl and add sugar and water. Cover the mixture and place it in the refrigerator until it forms a sauce.

MANDARIN BREAD PUDDING

"This recipe features that favorite flavor pairing inspired by the Droste chocolate oranges I received from my parents every holiday" explains co-owner Lisa Ritter. Both she and Mary Odson of Big Sugar love this combination of dark chocolate and orange.

YIELD: 8 SERVINGS

2 large	eggs	1/2 ounce	Grand Marnier liqueur (optional)
2 1/4 cups	half-and-half	2 cups	day-old, sliced white bread
1/2 cup	granulated sugar	2/3 cup	dark chocolate, chopped coarsely
1 teaspoon	vanilla extract		unsalted butter, softened,
1/4 teaspoon	kosher salt		for greasing baking dish
1 teaspoon	orange zest*		

If not using Grand Marnier liqueur, use 2 teaspoons of zest.

Preheat oven to 350°F.

Beat the eggs lightly in a small bowl. Place the beaten eggs, half-and-half, sugar, vanilla extract, salt, orange zest and Grand Marnier liqueur (if using) in a large mixing bowl and whisk to combine. Tear the bread slices into squares, roughly 2-by-2 inches, and add them to the egg mixture, stirring gently to moisten the bread completely.

Spoon the mixture into a greased, oven-proof, 8-by-8-inch glass baking dish. Scatter the chopped chocolate over the top of the bread mixture and use a spoon to distribute the chocolate evenly throughout the mixture.

Create a water bath by placing the baking dish in a larger heat-proof pan and filling the pan with hot water halfway up the side of the baking dish.

Carefully transfer the baking dish to the oven and bake for 45 to 50 minutes or until a knife inserted in the center of the pudding comes out clean. Use extreme care when removing the pudding from the water bath, and leave it in the oven until it has cooled and can be removed safely.

Serve the pudding warm with freshly whipped cream and garnish with a piece of orange peel.

Enjoy.

The Big Sugar Bakeshop, located in Studio City and nestled among some fantastic boutiques, is a kid-friendly stop for some home-style sweets. Baking sweet treats daily that are made with only quality ingredients, the Big Sugar kitchen staff have become authorities on cookies, pies, cakes and fudge.

Especially good are the "doughnut muffins" rolled in cinnamon sugar, and the peanut butter buckeyes.

The shop, which has a quaint, antique look, offers gift items as well.

The House of Blues opened on Sunset Strip in 1994 in the heart of West Hollywood. Originally founded by Isaac Tigrett and Dan Aykroyd as a home for soul food and great music, the nightclub showcases a music hall, retail store and the members-only Foundation Room.

With skyline views of Los Angeles and a friendly, down-home atmosphere, it's the ultimate dining and music experience for lovers of contemporary jazz, gospel and rock. Brunch offerings on Sundays include live gospel music with soulful Southern food such as boiled shrimp, Creole jambalaya, omelets, cheese grits, and of course, the well known White Chocolate Banana Bread Pudding.

HOUSE OF BLUES

WHITE CHOCOLATE BANANA BREAD PUDDING

When House of Blues founder Isaac Tigrett picked up an old corrugated-metal farm building in South Carolina and moved it to Los Angeles to become the home for his House of Blues, many thought he was an eccentric. When he introduced his guests to this soulful bread pudding, they realized that the delightful mix of music and dessert was destined for greatness on the Hollywood Strip.

YIELD: 12 SERVINGS

BREAD PUDDING

12 large	egg yolks		1 teaspoon	vanilla extract
3 cups	granulated sugar		6 1/4 cups	French bread cubes with crusts
3 cups	whole milk		4 1/4 cups	French bread cubes without crusts
3 cups	heavy cream		1 1/2	bananas, cut into 1/4-inch slices
13 ounces	white chocolate			

Preheat oven to 275°F.

In stainless steel mixing bowl, combine the egg yolks and sugar until blended. Set the mixture aside.

In a large saucepan bring the milk and cream to a boil over high heat. Immediately turn off the heat when a boil is reached. Add the white chocolate and the vanilla to the saucepan and stir until the chocolate melts and the entire mixture is smooth.

Slowly stir in the 1/3 cup of the egg-yolk-and-sugar mixture to the milk-and-cream mixture to temper it. Then slowly stir in the remainder of the egg yolks and sugar.

Add the bread cubes and banana slices to the liquid and toss to coat the bread cubes and distribute the banana slices uniformly. Set this aside for 20 minutes to allow the bread cubes to absorb the liquid.

Meanwhile, grease either twelve 6-ounce ramekins or one 9-by13-inch baking pan. If using ramekins, place them on a baking sheet.

Place the bread pudding in the ramekins or the baking pan and bake for 45 minutes. Then rotate the baking sheet or pan 180 degrees and bake for another 30 minutes, or until the pudding is golden brown.

At serving time, drizzle chocolate sauce (page 90) on top of pudding.

You may also spoon some whiskey sauce (page 91) on the bottom of the serving plate.

BRIOCHE BREAD PUDDING

Making bread pudding was once considered the clever cook's strategy for using leftover or stale bread. Today it's become a reason to buy the bread and allow it to sit for a day or so before use. This rich and dense chocolate version uses brioche bread, and is included courtesy of Ramon Perez of Comme Ça. The pudding will tempt anyone to indulge in a second helping.

YIELD: 12 SERVINGS

BANANA PUREE

1/4 cup	mashed banana	1 teaspoon	orange juice
1 teaspoon	granulated sugar		

In a small bowl, combine the mashed banana, sugar and orange juice. Set aside.

PUDDING

2 cups	heavy cream	1/4 cup	banana puree
3/4 cup	64 per cent dark chocolate	2 cups	1-inch cubes of brioche
2 large	eggs	1/2 cup	medium-chopped,
4 large	egg yolks		64 per cent chocolate
1/2 cup	granulated sugar		

Preheat oven to 350°F.

Pour the cream into a medium saucepan and, over medium-high-heat, bring to a boil.

Reduce heat and add the 3/4 cup of chocolate, whisking constantly until the mixture is smooth.

In a medium mixing bowl, whisk the eggs, egg yolks, sugar and banana puree until they are blended. Add this to the cream-and-chocolate mixture and stir until blended.

Add the brioche cubes and toss to coat them in the cream and chocolate. Remove from heat and allow to cool.

Add the 1/2 cup of chopped chocolate and stir. Place this mixture into a greased 8-by-8-inch baking pan or muffin pans. Bake for approximately 15 minutes or until custard is set. Serve immediately.

This modern French brasserie, opened in 2007 by chef David Myers, conveys the feeling of being in Paris or New York. Before opening Comme Ça, Meyers worked with Charlie Trotter in Chicago and Daniel Boulud in New York City as well as Joachim Splichal in Los Angeles.

With his classic take on traditional style, Myers has helped make seriously good food one of the prime attractions of trendy Melrose Avenue. The understated interior design is mostly black and white, with a few homey touches such as antique mirrors and books. The complex and unique flavors with a French flair, along with a comfortable, romantic setting make this must stop place in Los Angeles.

In this Brioche Bread Pudding chocolate and cream have been paired and then trickily balanced with banana puree. It's a dessert that's perfect for sharing.

Pink Lady Apple Crostata
with Caramel Sauce

"I think my favorite fruit of the year is an apple, Pink Lady apples in particular," says pastry chef Christina Olufson. She finds this rustic-style tart hard to resist wrapped in its sugar-coated crust, warmed from the oven and drizzled with caramel sauce. A|O|C is a casual, european-style wine bar and restaurant co-owned by chef Suzanne Goin and Caroline Styne.

YIELD: 8-10 SERVINGS

DOUGH

2 cups	all purpose flour	1/4 cup	ice water
1 teaspoon	kosher salt	1/4 cup	heavy cream
1/4 cup	granulated sugar		
8 ounces (2 sticks)	cold, unsalted butter, cubed into 1/2-inch cubes		

Place the flour, salt and granulated sugar into a food processor and pulse two or three times to combine. Add the butter and pulse three or four more times, until the butter is in pea-size pieces. Add the ice water and pulse three or four more times. The dough will start to come together, but will still be very crumbly. Bring the dough together into a disk-shape, enclose in plastic wrap and chill for 1 hour, or overnight.

THE APPLES

3 (about 1 pound)	medium-size apples, peeled, cored and cut into 1/4-inch slices	4 tablespoons (1/2 stick)	unsalted butter
		2 tablespoons	granulated sugar

Place the butter into a small saucepan and melt it over medium heat. Continue to cook the butter until it lightly browns, releasing a nutty aroma. Pour the melted butter over the sliced apples. Sprinkle the granulated sugar over the apples as well, and toss to combine.

THE CROSTATA (the chilled dough)

1 1/2 cup	natural apple sauce	2 tablespoons	granulated sugar
1/4 cup	heavy cream		

Line a 9-by-13-inch baking sheet with parchment paper. Roll the chilled dough and place it onto the parchment paper. Spread the apple sauce onto the center of the dough, being careful to leave a 4-inch border of dough uncovered.

Place the sliced-apple mixture over the apple sauce, allowing the slices to fall naturally into place. Fold the uncovered dough over the slices, Refrigerate the crostata for 30 minutes before baking. (You may also build the crostata ahead of time and freeze it, then bake when needed.)

Preheat the oven to 450°F.

Remove the crostata from the refrigerator or freezer. Brush the cream onto the crust, covering any exposed dough. Sprinkle the granulated sugar over the cream-coated crust. This will give the crust

(Continued at left)

(Continued from right)
a caramelized color during baking. Bake for 45 minutes to 1 hour, until the apples are tender and the crust is a deep golden brown. Allow the crostata to cool on a wire rack.

VANILLA CARAMEL SAUCE*

1 cup	granulated sugar
1/4 cup	light corn syrup
1 cup	water
1 each	vanilla pod, split and scraped for seeds
1 1/4 cup	heavy cream
2 tablespoons	unsalted butter
	vanilla ice cream

*The sauce can be made and kept up to a week in advance.

Combine the sugar, corn syrup, water and vanilla pod and seeds into a medium sauce pan over high heat. In a separate saucepan combine the cream and butter and heat until the butter is just melted. Continue cooking the sugar mixture until it becomes amber in color. Slowly add the cream mixture, whisking to incorporate. Continue whisking until all of the cream is added. Cool slightly. Remove the vanilla pod and discard. Set the sauce aside until the crostata is ready to serve.

To serve, cut the crostata into 8 to 10 equal slices and place each slice on a plate. Spoon some of the caramel sauce all over the crostata slices and onto the plate. Place a scoop of ice cream on top or next to the slice.

The crostata may be stored in the refrigerator for up to three days. It may be reheated in the oven at 350°F. for 8 to 10 minutes.

Mrs. Knott's Boysenberry Pie

Just how this famous pie came to be is a story of how much of Los Angeles developed. Start with a dream, an idea, something of a plan, nice neighbors, and lots of fire in the belly and you end up with a new food and a signature to anchor this dream in the minds (and bellies) of your friends and pleasure-seekers alike.

Note: Before preparing the pie-filling recipe below, prepare a 9-inch, two-crust pie shell from the recipe on page 90.

YIELD: 6 SERVINGS

7 1/2 ounces	water		3 tablespoons	corn starch
dash	salt		2 ounces (1/4 cup)	water
3/4 cup, plus 1 tablespoon	granulated Sugar			powdered sugar,
1 tablespoon	corn syrup			for garnish
1 teaspoon	lemon juice			
16 ounces	frozen boysenberries*			
	(do not thaw)			

Frozen blackberries or raspberries may be substituted for boysenberries.

Preheat the oven to 400°F.

In a saucepan, combine the 7 1/2 ounces of water, salt, sugar, corn syrup and lemon juice. Bring mixture to a boil and set it aside.

Place the unthawed frozen boysenberries or blackberries in a large mixing bowl, separating the individual berries as much as possible.

Dissolve the corn starch in the 1/4 cup water and pour this over the berries in the mixing bowl.

Add the mixture of sugar, corn starch and lemon juice to the mixing bowl with the frozen berries and stir everything well.

Pour the berry mixture onto the bottom crust of the prepared 9-inch pie shell. Cover with the top crust. Seal the edges of the two crusts with the tines of a fork or pinch the edges to seal closed. Make several 3-inch slashes across the center of the top crust to release steam while baking.

Bake the pie on an oven rack in the middle position for 40 minutes or until the crust turns golden brown. Cool on a rack.

Before serving the pie, the top crust may be dusted with powdered sugar.

As a young man with four young children during the 1920s, Walter Knott and a cousin began a berry farm in bucolic Buena Park, Calif., and began selling their harvests in a roadside stand. They later expanded with a small restaurant where they sold their pies.

In the 1930s Walter Knott visited a farm maintained by Rudolph Boysen, who had cross-cultivated loganberries, blackberries and red raspberries to produce a larger fruit, which would come to be known as the boysenberry. Mrs. Cordelia Knott decided the new berry might draw customers to the roadside business and added boysenberry pie to the offerings in its tea room. It quickly became a favorite of the restaurant's customers.

The year 1940 saw further expansion with the addition of a 'Wild West Ghost Town and Railway,' filled with a pan-for-gold attraction, a cable car, a mine ride and a shooting gallery. In succeeding decades, the park continued expanding. Today it is one of the most popular amusement parks in the United States.

Jar is a contemporary chophouse in the heart of Los Angeles featuring the cuisine of one of Bravo channel's Top Chef Masters, Suzanne Tracht. The interior is simple, warm and cozy in the style of formal supper clubs.

The signature pot roast with carmelized onions and carrots keeps customers coming back, and the Sunday brunch is one of the best Los Angeles has to offer. Other quality sides include pea tendrils, sautéed chanterelles and water spinach.

(Continued from right)

milk in to the egg mixture, then whisk rapidly to incorporate the eggs without curdling the mixture.

Return the mixture to the milk remaining in the saucepan. Cook over medium-low heat, stirring constantly, until the mixture becomes thick and bubbly, 6 to 8 minutes. Cover with plastic wrap, pressing it flat across the pastry cream's surface so no skin forms. Refrigerate for 1 hour or until chilled.

ASSEMBLY

	Pastry Cream
	Tart Shells
1/2 cup	whipping cream, whipped to soft peaks, divided
4	ripe bananas, sliced 1/4 inch thick

Place about 1 tablespoon of pastry cream in bottom of each shell. In large mixing bowl, fold the remaining pastry cream in with 3/4 of the whipped cream. Gently fold in the bananas. Fill each shell just to top. Place large dollop of whipped cream on top to cover.

JAR
BANANA CREAM PIE

Few flavor pairings are as satisfying as bananas and cream. This is simply a wonderful dessert from Suzanne Tracht's Restaurant, Jar.

YIELD: 8 SERVINGS

PASTRY DOUGH

2 1/4 cups plus 2 tablespoons	all purpose flour (plus more for rolling)	4 large	egg yolks
1/2 cup	granulated sugar	4 to 5 tablespoons	heavy cream
1 cup	unsalted butter, cubed and chilled, plus more for buttering tart pans		non-stick cooking spray

Combine the flour and sugar in food processor or mixer. With machine running, slowly add the butter, and process or mix until you have a fine meal. Mix together the egg yolks and cream, and slowly add them to the flour mixture. Process or mix until the dough just starts to come together.

Turn the dough onto a floured work surface. Work the dough with the heel of your palm until it comes together flat and smooth. Form the dough into eight small disks. Wrap the disks of dough in plastic wrap and refrigerate them for 2 hours.

Butter eight 4-inch tart pans. (If you have only 4 pans, you can make two batches of four tart shells at a time.) Roll the disks out to 1/8 inch thick. Form dough into the tart pans. With a rolling pin, roll over the tops of the pans until the excess dough drops from the sides. Press the dough gently to the sides of the pans. You must chill and weigh down the dough. The easiest way is by spraying a paper coffee filter with cooking spray and filling it with dried beans, then placing it on top of the dough. Chill the shells for at least another 2 hours.

Preheat oven to 400°F

Bake the tart shells (with the paper coffee filter bags and beans still on top) until they become light amber, 15 to 20 minutes. Remove the filters and let the tart shells cool to room temperature, then carefully remove the shells from the pans.

PASTRY CREAM

7 large	egg yolks	1/4 cup	all purpose flour
1/2 cup	granulated sugar	2 cups	whole milk
4 tablespoons	cornstarch	1	vanilla bean, split and scraped

Beat egg yolks and sugar until mixture is pale and forms ribbons when the beaters are lifted from the bowl. Sift in the cornstarch and flour, mixing well.

Heat the milk in a saucepan over medium heat. Split and scrape the vanilla bean and place the pod and seeds in the milk. Once the milk comes to a boil, remove the bean, slowly whisk about 1/4 of the *(Continued at left)*

MEXICAN CHOCOLATE CREAM PIE

From the kitchen of Mary Sue Milliken and Susan Feniger comes this quick and easy pie which combines the flavors of cinnamon, chocolate, cream and almonds over a meringue crust. The pie is topped with dark chocolate 'curls' which then take center stage.

YIELD: 8 TO 10 SERVINGS

1/2 cup	slivered almonds		2 1/4 cups	heavy cream, chilled
3 large	egg whites		1/3 cup	powdered sugar
3/4 cup	granulated sugar		1/4 teaspoon	(or to taste) ground cinnamon
1/2 teaspoon	cream of tartar		1/4 teaspoon	vanilla extract
7 ounces	semisweet chocolate, chopped		2 to 3 ounces	bittersweet chocolate, grated or shaved into curls for garnish
1 ounce	unsweetened chocolate, chopped			

Preheat the oven to 350°F.

Spread the almonds on a cookie sheet and roast in the oven until golden, about 5 to 10 minutes. Set aside to cool.

Turn the oven down to 275°F.

Butter the bottom and sides (not the lip) of a 9-inch glass pie plate.

Place the egg whites in the bowl of an electric mixer and set over a pan of hot tap water until the bowl is slightly warmed. Then whisk the warm egg whites until soft peaks form. Whisk in the cream of tartar and then add the granulated sugar in a slow, steady stream, whisking continuously. Continue whisking until stiff and glossy, about 5 to 10 minutes longer.

Make a pie shell with the meringue by smoothing it over the bottom and sides of the buttered pie plate. Bake until the meringue is slightly crisp and dry, about 40 to 50 minutes. Cool on a rack.

Combine the two chocolates in a bowl over simmering water, and stir occasionally until melted. Let cool to room temperature.

Combine the heavy cream, powdered sugar, cinnamon, and vanilla in a mixing bowl. Beat at medium speed until very soft peaks form, about 2 to 3 minutes. Stir one-third of the whipped cream mixture into the melted chocolates to lighten them. Then add that mixture to the remaining whipped cream and gently fold in until completely incorporated.

Scatter the toasted almonds over the cooked meringue shell. Top with the chocolate cream filling, smoothing the top. Decorate the top with the grated chocolate or chocolate curls. Cover and refrigerate at least 1 hour before serving.

The Border Grill restaurant in Santa Monica, whose specialty is the home cooking of Oaxaca and the Yucatan, is another venture for two of Los Angeles' favorite chefs, Mary Sue Milliken and Susan Feniger (known as the 'Too Hot Tamales'). The restaurant serves upscale, modern Mexican food in this hip, urban cantina setting.

Their love of Latin American food can be seen in the way they think of colors in food terms – olive green, mustard yellow and cayenne red, dominate the food and decor.

Milliken and Feniger are into having fun with food and serving it in a fun style. So they've added their talents to the gourmet food truck phenomenon that has cropped up in American cities with their Border Grill Truck. It's an exciting and splashy way to bring their creative new takes on traditional Mexican flavors to the Los Angeles area's neighborhoods, a recognition that "bringing the restaurant to you" has caught on fast with lovers of Mexican food.

The Hollywood crowd loves the sweet moments found at Sweet Lady Jane, which has been serving Los Angeles for more than 20 years with high-quality desserts.

After baking for area restaurants in her home, and acquiring a reputation for quality products, Jane Lockhart opened Sweet Lady Jane bakery and restaurant on Melrose Avenue.

Lockhart became a baker after she discovered that by preparing desserts with the freshest ingredients and the utmost care could result in sweet dishes that were moist, not too sweet and absolutely delicious.

Known as "the cake designer to the stars," Lockhart has been known to prepare such unusual creations as an entire wedding cake of cheesecake and a vegan red velvet wedding cake.

In addition to the cakes, pies, brownies, cookies, breakfast pastries and tarts, Sweet Lady Jane's offers lunch sandwiches served on house-made breads and rolls.

To mark those most important occasions or simply to satisfy an afternoon craving, Lockhart's desserts answer the call.

RASPBERRY CHEESECAKE

This cheesecake is a treat for both the eye and the palate. Raspberries are found throughout the cake, and whole ones can also be used to create a colorful topping or to garnish each serving.

YIELD: 9-INCH CAKE

GRAHAM CRACKER CRUST

1 2/3 cup	graham crackers, crushed to fine crumb	3 tablespoons	granulated sugar
		8 tablespoons (1 stick)	unsalted butter, melted

Preheat the oven to 350°F.

In a medium mixing bowl blend the cracker crumbs with the sugar. Add the melted butter and mix well. Using a 9-inch spring-form pan, press the crumb mixture onto the bottom of the pan and approximately 1 inch up the sides. Bake for 12 minutes. Remove the crust from the oven and allow it to cool.

CHEESECAKE FILLING*

20 ounces	cream cheese, softened to room temperature	3 tablespoons	all purpose flour
		1/2 tablespoon	pure vanilla extract
1/3 cup	granulated sugar	3 tablespoons	heavy cream
3 medium	eggs	1 pint	raspberries, fresh or frozen

In a medium mixing bowl, blend the softened cream cheese and the sugar until all of the sugar is incorporated and the mixture is smooth. Add the eggs one at a time to the cream cheese and mix until each is incorporated. Add the flour and mix well. Then add the vanilla extract and blend well. Finally, add the cream to blend. Do not over-mix. By hand, crush the pint of fresh or frozen raspberries and, with a spoon, fold the berries into the cheesecake mixture.

RASPBERRY SYRUP

1 pint	raspberries, fresh or frozen	whipped cream for serving,
1/4 cup	granulated sugar	optional
	fresh whole raspberries for garnish, optional	

In a small saucepan, cook the second pint of raspberries with the sugar until the berries release a syrup and the fruit cooks down. Strain the syrup into a small bowl and allow it to cool.

Fill a small plastic bag with the syrup. Make a tiny cut in the tip of one bottom corner of the plastic bag. Gently squeeze out the syrup, creating concentric circles on top of the cheesecake. Then, with a sharp knife, pull through the lines of the raspberry syrup circles every inch or so to form a pattern of points in the concentric circles.

Bake for approximately one hour. Cool on a rack for several hours before refrigerating. Chill overnight. At serving time, you may want to top the cheesecake with a few whole berries and also add a dollop of whipped cream to each serving.

Recipe modified for the home cook

CHOCOLATE CHEESECAKE SANDWICH

Terri Blumgarden of Canter's is always looking for a new approach to old favorites. She presented this cheesecake sandwich at a culinary competition for desserts. Although it did not win the competition, it did win some new friends and customers for the deli.

YIELD: 8

GRAHAM CRACKER CRUST

1 1/2 cups	graham cracker crumbs	5 tablespoons	unsalted butter
1/4 cup	granulated sugar		

Preheat oven to 350°F.

In a mixing bowl combine the graham cracker crumbs, granulated sugar and butter until blended. Firmly press the mixture into the bottom of a 8-inch-square pan.

Bake for 8 to 10 minutes until golden brown.

CHEESECAKE

8 ounces	cream cheese	2 large	eggs
4 ounces	farmers cheese*	1/2 cup	sour cream
1/2 cup	granulated sugar	1 cup	mini chocolate chips
1/2 teaspoon	vanilla extract		

*cottage cheese or ricotta cheese may be used.

Preheat oven to 300°F.

In a large mixing bowl, combine the cream cheese and farmer's cheese until the mixture is soft and fluffy. Add sugar and vanilla and beat until all the ingredients are well blended. While continuing to mix the ingredients, gradually add the eggs, one at a time and then fold in the sour cream until everything is blended.

Place the mixture over the graham cracker crust and distribute the chocolate chips evenly over the top. Bake for 45 to 55 minutes. Turn oven off and allow the cheesecake to cool in the oven. Refrigerate overnight.

TO ASSEMBLE CHEESECAKE

2	slices of Challah or egg bread	1 tablespoon	unsalted butter, divided
2	thin slices of cheddar cheese		
2	slices of cheesecake, 4 inches by 2 inches and 1/2 inch thick		

Butter one slice of egg bread and place it in medium size skillet, buttered side down. Place one slice of the cheddar cheese on the bread and then place two slices of cheesecake on top of the cheddar,

(Continued at right)

For more than 80 years Canter's Delicatessen, a classic mid-century diner, has been a favorite hangout for locals, show-biz personalities and visitors alike. The place never closes, and it often caters to the TV and movie studio crowd, serving such traditional deli foods as pastrami, corned beef, matzoh ball soup, and lox and bagels. Movies have been filmed here and celebrities frequently pop in for a 3 a.m. nosh.

Canter's has enjoyed continuous expansion since its opening in 1931. The Kibbitz Room, adjacent to the main dining room, opened in the 1961 with live bands playing nightly. Thus began its special appeal to the trendy young set.

Something of a Los Angeles institution, it's one of the largest delis in the United States.

When paying the bill, it's hard to pass up the desserts display window and not pick up a little something to take home.

(Continued from left)
with the chocolate-chip toppings facing each other. Place another slice of cheddar on top of the cheesecake and then place the second slice of bread on top to form the sandwich. Butter the top of the sandwich. Cook on medium heat until crispy brown and then turn over to crisp the other side. Slice the sandwich diagonally.

Garnish each serving with some shaved chocolate or chocolate chips.

When Walt Disney opened the original Disneyland amusement park in 1955 in Anaheim, California, the original Carnation Café on the park's Main Street USA opened with it. It remains today a full-service restaurant with bright red-and-white-striped café umbrellas adding to the festive spirit.

This distinctly American-style café still serves basic American food—pot pies, baked-potato soup, butcher-block sandwiches, old-fashioned banana splits and Mickey Mouse waffles.

The bakery next door is sure to please with these classic oatmeal raisin cookies.

OATMEAL-RAISIN COOKIES

Here's an old-fashioned favorite from the "Happiest Place on Earth" – Disneyland. The recipe is easy and quick to prepare, and the cookies are a great snack food. You also can take them to a new level by substituting dried cranberries or cherries for the raisins.

YIELD: APPROXIMATELY 24 COOKIES

3 1/2 cups	all purpose flour	1 3/4 cup	brown sugar, packed
1 tablespoon	baking powder	1 1/2 cups	granulated sugar
1 1/2 teaspoons	ground cinnamon	3 large	eggs
1 teaspoon	salt	1 teaspoon	vanilla
1 teaspoon	baking soda	4 cups	rolled oats
2 cups plus 2 tablespoons	shortening	2 1/2 cups	raisins

Preheat the oven to 350°F.

In a medium mixing bowl, blend the flour, baking powder, cinnamon, salt and baking soda. Set aside.

In a large mixing bowl, blend the shortening, brown sugar, granulated sugar, eggs and vanilla until fluffy. Add the flour and baking powder mixture to the shortening mixture and combine until everything is well blended, about 2 minutes. Stir in the oats and raisins to finish making the dough.

Divide the dough into approximately 24 balls, each containing about 2 1/2 tablespoons (about the size of an ice cream scoop). Place each ball on a baking sheet and press down until the dough is about 1/4-inch thick and about 3 inches in diameter. The cookies should be separated by about 2 inches.

Bake for 9 to 12 minutes. Cool on the baking sheet.

GRACE RESTAURANT

Doughnut Shoppe

These doughnuts are a signature dessert at Grace, and you'll sometimes find diners there who've come just for them, lending the restaurant an identity as a dessert destination. The doughnuts can also be fried in a ball shape and filled with custard, butterscotch, chocolate, lemon, etc.

YIELD: APPROXIMATELY 24 DOUGHNUTS

3 1/8 tablespoons	active dry yeast	1 5/8 ounce	dry milk
13 ounces	warm water	8 cups	all purpose flour
3 large	eggs	7 ounces	unsalted butter at
1 cup	granulated sugar		room temperature
1/2 teaspoon	salt		

Place the yeast in the bowl of an electric mixer. Pour the water over the yeast and allow it to sit for a few minutes. In a large bowl combine all of the dry ingredients. Whisk together the yeast and the water until the yeast is completely dissolved. Add the eggs and whisk again to combine. Add the dry ingredients to the yeast mixture. Using the mixer's hook attachment, mix the ingredients on low speed until a ball starts to form. Switch mixer to medium speed and mix for 6 to 7 minutes. You want the dough to become smooth and elastic.

Add the butter and mix until the butter is completely emulsified. The dough should be supple, not greasy. Place the dough in a large greased bowl and cover with plastic wrap. Place in a warm spot to double in bulk. When it has doubled, gently deflate and allow to double once more. Once the dough has doubled again, gently turn out onto a clean work surface sprinkled with flour. Cut the doughnuts into desired size. Cut holes into the doughnuts (if desired, you may leave some of the doughnuts whole to be used as filled doughnuts).

Fill a large pot no more than halfway with canola oil and heat the oil to 350°F. Be very careful when working with hot oil. Once the oil has reached 350° gently drop the doughnuts into the oil. Using a spoon, carefully baste the tops of the doughnuts with hot oil. Once the tops start to puff, flip the doughnuts. Skewers work well for this. Once again, carefully baste the tops of the doughnuts a few times. Allow the doughnuts to fry until they are medium golden brown on one side. Flip once more and allow the other side to become golden brown. Carefully remove the doughnuts from the oil and place them on paper towels.

If you are glazing the doughnuts, place each warm doughnut in the desired glaze. For sugar coatings, simply toss warm doughnuts in sugar.

GLAZING THE DOUGHNUTS

1 3/4 cups	sifted powdered sugar	2 ounces	heavy cream
3/4 cup	Meyer lemon juice		

Place all ingredients in a bowl and combine them until the mixture becomes smooth. Adjust the taste and consistency of the glaze as needed. While the doughnuts are warm, dip them in the glaze to cover.

(Continued at right)

One dictionary defines the word grace as "beauty of form, being right and proper and being generous or thoughtful of others," and it perfectly describes the contemporary American bistro founded by chef Neal Fraser and his wife Amy.

Fraser is the first California chef to win the coveted Iron Chef America competition after outscoring chef Cat Cora.

Not to be missed is Fraser's braised pork shank and beet salad with pistachios. It's a dish reminiscent of old Hollywood charm.

Grace is consistently named one of the best restaurants in Los Angeles.

(Continued from left)

FILLING THE DOUGHNUTS

If you'd like to fill the doughnuts, toss them in sugar while they're warm. Then, holding a doughnut in your hand, carefully insert the star tip of a filled pastry bag into it. Gently squeeze the bag to fill the doughnut. You'll feel it swell slightly as you fill it.

Sugar-coating the doughnuts:

Here are a few sugar mixes that may be used for coating the doughnuts:

Cinnamon sugar:
2 tablespoons granulated sugar, 2 teaspoons cinnamon.

Cocoa sugar:
2 tablespoons granulated sugar, 1 tablespoon cocoa powder, 1 teaspoon cinnamon, 1/4 teaspoon salt.

Curried sugar:
3 tablespoons granulated sugar, 1/4 teaspoon salt, 1 teaspoon ground ginger, 1 teaspoon cinnamon, 1 teaspoon sweet curry powder.

Here is a simple little cookie, with a crisp, pie-like dough, and added sweetness from the granulated sugar sprinkled on top. It is designed to complement a rich, creamy dessert such as the panna cotta with blackberry compote by adding to each silky mouthful a delightful crunch.

FRENCH BUTTER COOKIES

A simple little cookie to compliment a rich dessert.

YIELD: APPROXIMATELY 24 COOKIES

1 3/4 cups	cake flour	2 tablespoons	dark brown sugar
3/4 cup	all purpose flour	1/4 teaspoon	kosher salt
16 tablespoons (2 sticks)	unsalted butter, softened		granulated sugar for topping
1/2 cup	confectioner's sugar		

Preheat oven to 350°F.

Sift the flour and set it aside.

If using a hand mixer, first place the butter, confectioner's sugar, brown sugar and salt in a large mixing bowl. Cream the mixture until it is combined, about 30 seconds to 1 minute. With the mixer off, add one third of the flour mixture and mix well. Repeat in two more batches with the remaining two thirds of the flour.

If using a stand mixer fitted with a paddle attachment, place the butter, confectioner's sugar, brown sugar and salt in the bowl. On low speed, cream the mixture until it is combined, about 30 seconds. With the mixer off, add one third of the flour mixture. Turn the mixture on low speed and paddle for 10 more seconds. Repeat in two more batches with the remaining two thirds of the flour. Scrape down the sides and the bottom of the bowl, using a spatula and paddle the dough for 10 more seconds.

Remove the dough from the mixer bowl and place it on a flat work surface. Form it into a 5-inch disk. Wrap the dough in plastic wrap and chill in the refrigerator for 1 hour. When the dough is well chilled, divide it in half. Working with half the dough at a time, flour the work surface and roll the dough with a rolling pin to 1/8 inch thick. Using a round 2 1/2 inch diameter cutter (our cutter of your choice), cut as many cookies as you can get. With a spatula, transfer the cookies to a parchment-lined cookie sheet, spacing them 1/2 inch apart. Repeat with the remaining dough (you can re-roll the dough once). Sprinkle granulated sugar very generously on the cookies and place them in the oven. The cookies should bake for about 15 minutes and are done when lightly golden. Let them cool on the baking sheet.

Briouats (Moroccan Cookies)

دار المغرب
DAR MAGHREB

Briouats are small, crispy Moroccan pastries filled with a sweet almond mixture. For each briouat, a bit of the filling mixture is placed on a long strip of phyllo dough, which is then folded into a triangle in much the same way as a flag is folded. These are a deliciously light finish to a hearty meal. Enjoy with traditional mint tea (page 91).

YIELD: 24 COOKIES

FILLING FOR PHYLLO-DOUGH TRIANGLES

8 ounces	raw, shelled almonds		1/4 cup	fresh orange juice
2 tablespoons	vegetable oil		6 sheets	phyllo dough,
1/2 cup	granulated sugar			each approximately
1/2 teaspoon	cinnamon			12-by-17 inches
1 tablespoon	rose water*		1 large	egg, beaten
1 teaspoon	melted, unsalted butter			

Rose water is available at specialty markets or in the herbs or vitamin sections of some supermarkets.

Prehead over to 350°F.

Lightly toss the almonds with oil to coat them. Place them in a medium-size skillet and roast them until golden brown and fragrant. Allow 5 to 8 minutes.

Coarsely grind the almonds in a food process or chop them finely.

In a medium mixing bowl, combine the almonds, sugar, cinnamon, rose water, butter and orange juice. Mix everything thoroughly until the ingredients reach the consistency of a smooth paste.

TO MAKE THE BRIOUAT TRIANGLES

On a flat work surface, cut one sheet of phyllo dough lengthwise into 3-inch-wide strips. Set the strips aside. Cover the remaining sheets of phyllo dough with a damp cloth until ready to use.

Roll a bit of the filling into a very small ball, about one inch in diameter.

Place the ball about 1 inch above the bottom edge of one strip of phyllo dough and fold the bottom edge to just cover the filling, creating a plump square.

Fold the bottom left corner of the square up to align with the right edge of the dough. You should now have the beginning of your first 'triangle'.

Then fold the bottom right corner of the strip up to the left edge of the dough.

Continue folding, right and then left, until you reach the end of the dough.

Using a small pastry brush, 'seal' the plump triangle with some of the beaten egg.

Follow the same procedure for the other sheets of phyllo dough.

(Continued at right)

Dar Maghreb's guests enter the restaurant through beautiful brass-plated doors and into another world, with a sky lit courtyard and a bubbling fountain. The late owner, Pierre Dupart, designed this magnificent space, a re-creation of a 15th century Koranic school in Fez, Morocco. Dupart's love of exotic architecture is apparent throughout Dar Maghreb. After ordering your drink, your hands are washed with warm water and you're given a towel to serve as your napkin. You are then presented with such traditional Moroccan dishes as b'stilla (flaky pastry filled with chicken, almonds and eggs and powdered sugar and cinnamon on top), lamb with honey, couscous, cookies and mint tea.

Adding a sensual element are the belly dancers and soft pillows. Most dishes are eaten with fingers only, conforming to Moroccan tradition.

(Continued from left)
TO FRY AND SERVE THE BRIOUAT COOKIES

3/4 cup	vegetable oil
1/2 cup	honey for dipping
1 tablespoon	sesame seeds, optional

In a 12-to-14-inch skillet, heat the 3/4 cup of vegetable oil on medium-low heat. Fry the triangles until they are golden brown, about 2 minutes, turning them over once. Do not crowd too many in the pan at one time.

Remove the triangles from the skillet with a slotted spoon, drain them on absorbent paper and allow them to cool.

Serve the briouats at room temperature or when they are still warm. Just before serving, dip each briouat in warmed honey. If desired, sprinkle each triangle lightly with toasted sesame seeds.

Leftover briouats can be stored in an airtight container at room temperature for up to one week. It is not advisable to store in the refrigerator as it will make the phyllo dough soggy.

BLD boasts lots of relaxed sidewalk seating for the casual dining crowd. They come for the house-cured salmon Benedict for breakfast, the blackened catfish or crab sandwich for lunch and the lamb burger for dinner. Of course, all three meals are served throughout the day and boxed food is available for Hollywood Bowl concerts and trips to the beach or park.

The minimalist, contemporary interior is quite impressive and an compatible background for the food being served. A collection of miniature kitchen appliances are displayed as art.

BLD

Caramel-Dipped Apples

B L D's Chef de Cuisine Diana Stavardis says she literally begged Pastry Chef Mariah Swan to add this luscious treat to the restaurant's fall dessert menu. It is served as a do-it-yourself plate holding three very small apples swathed in caramel and several fancy toppings for dipping each bite. The tartness of the apples combined with the sweetness of the caramel tinged with apple cider vinegar complete the satisfying taste profile. The toppings simply add to the experience.

YIELD: 1 serving of 3 apples

CARAMEL SAUCE

1 cup	granulated sugar	1/2 cup	heavy cream
1/3 cup	water	2 tablespoons	apple cider vinegar
1 1/2 teaspoon	light corn syrup		

While preparing the caramel, keep a pastry brush in ice water handy to wash away any sugar crystals that may form during cooking. In a medium saucepan, combine the sugar, water and corn syrup. Place over high heat and cook until the mixture turns a medium amber color, making sure that the sides of the pan are clean and free of any sugar. Remove the caramel from heat and slowly pour in the cream. (Be careful, as the caramel will bubble up and spit a little as the cream is added.) Lower the heat to medium and place the pot back on the burner. Whisk the cream into the caramel until the two are combined and the mixture is smooth. Whisk in the apple-cider vinegar. Remove from heat and allow to cool.

TO DIP AND SERVE THE APPLES

3 very small crisp, tart apples, such as empire	your choice of toppings, such as chocolate sprinkles, chopped toasted pecans,
3 lollipop or caramel apple sticks	chocolate chip cookie crumbs, etc.

Place each stick firmly into the bottom (blossom) end of each apple. Dip each apple into the cooled caramel sauce three or four times to generously coat it. Place the dipped apples on a plate along with the toppings of your choice. When serving, include a small steak knife and a fork alongside the plate so the apples may be cut and the pieces pressed onto the desired topping.

Option: Core and cut the apples into wedges, place a stick in each wedge and dip into the caramel sauce to coat it. Place on a plate with the toppings.

CRÊPES WITH CRÈME FRAÎCHE MOUSSE AND FRICASSEE OF FRUITS

Mélisse

Josiah Citrin

Rising star chef Josiah Citrin offers a fresh California twist to a classic French dessert. This recipe includes instructions for cooking the crêpes themselves in a home kitchen. However, pre-packaged crêpes may be substituted.

YIELD: 6

CRÊPES

1 cup	milk	2 tablespoons	grapeseed oil
1/3	vanilla bean, split and scraped	3 tablespoons	all-purpose flour
		3 1/2 tablespoons	granulated sugar
2 large	eggs		butter, to coat the
1 tablespoon	orange zest		pan or skillet
2 tablespoons	unsalted butter		

Note: The ingredient measurements are more than enough to make six crêpes. This is to allow the possibility that one or more of the crêpes will tear while being cooked.

In a medium mixing bowl, whisk together the milk, scraped vanilla bean and seeds, eggs and orange zest. In a separate bowl, combine the flour and sugar and whisk together to break up the flour. Add the flour and sugar to the milk-and-egg mixture. Place the butter and grapeseed oil in a small bowl and heat gently in a microwave oven. Stir the melted butter and oil, then slowly combine them with the flour-and-milk mixture to emulsify the batter. Refrigerate the batter for 1 to 2 hours. This allows the bubbles to subside so the crêpes will be less likely to tear during cooking.

Heat a small, non-stick skillet or crepe pan on low-to-medium heat. Add butter to coat. Using a 1-to-2-ounce ladle or cup, pour the batter onto the pan and swirl it around to cover the entire surface. Cook for 30 seconds, or until you see the edges brown and the middle is a little puffed up. Then turn the crepe over and cook for another 10 seconds. Remove it to a cutting board or other clean, flat surface. As you cook the crêpes, lay each one out flat so they all can cool. Continue until all of the batter is gone.

CRÈME FRAÎCHE MOUSSE

2 large	egg yolks	3 tablespoons	plain yogurt
3 tablespoons	granulated sugar	1/2 cup	crème fraiche
1 teaspoon	gelatin powder	1 cup	heavy cream, whipped
1/4 cup	water		to medium peak
1/4	lemon, juiced		

In a bowl over simmering water, whisk together the egg yolks and sugar until the mixture is thick and pale. Set aside. Sprinkle the gelatin powder over 1/4 cup of water and allow to sit for 4 to 5 minutes to dissolve the gelatin. Add the lemon juice to the gelatin and stir the mixture gently. Add this to the warm egg yolks and sugar and set aside to cool, whisking occasionally. Combine the
(Continued at right)

(Continued from left)
whipped cream, crème fraiche and yogurt and whip again to a medium peak. Fold this mixture into the cooled gelatin, egg yolks and sugar and refrigerate for about 30 minutes.

THE FRICASSÉE OF FRUIT

1 pint	strawberries, trimmed and quartered
1/8 cup	extra virgin olive oil
1/2	vanilla bean, split and scraped
1/3 cup	light brown sugar
1/2 cup	blueberries
	lemon, zested and juiced
1/2 cup	blackberries
1 pint	raspberries

Pre-heat a large skillet or saucepan. Place the strawberries in the skillet or pan, over low-to-medium heat, and toss them with olive oil, vanilla bean and brown sugar. Add the blueberries and lemon zest and juice. (If the sugar begins to harden, add a little more water.) Do not over-cook the fruit. It should be just warm, not soft. Turn off the heat, add the blackberries and raspberries and gently toss them with the strawberries for about 10 seconds, being careful not to bruise or crush the raspberries. Check the sweetness. The mixture may need a little more sugar or lemon juice.

To serve, place each crepe on a plate and fill the center with the mousse, then fold in both sides of the crepe to form a roll. Top with the fruit fricassee.

Gino Angelini raises the approachable and flavorful home cooking up a notch or two with his classic osteria. The restaurant is a reflection of Angelini himself – warm and free from pretension. And its welcoming interior conveys the feeling of the small osterias found in the town squares of Italy.

The dishes Angelini prepares are all his own, and they mirror his expertise in traditional Italian cooking. He uses only quality ingredients and gives them a bit of family-style warmth. An example is his version of Nonna Elvira's (grandmother's) hand-made spinach pasta.

Many consider Angelini the best Italian chef in Los Angeles. He has fed, movie stars, heads of state, and famous musicians.

This mascarpone with mascerated pineapple, a touch of Grand Marnier liqueur and whipped egg whites and cheese add a light finale to any meal.

GLASS OF MASCARPONE
WITH PINEAPPLE

This is a refreshing and light dessert to be enjoyed with a little dessert wine and good company.

YIELD: 4 SERVINGS

1	whole pineapple, with leaves reserved		2 large	egg whites
			2 tablespoons	granulated sugar
4 tablespoons	Grand Marnier liqueur		5 ounces	mascarpone cheese

Cut the leaves from the pineapple and set them aside for garnish.

Cut the skin from the pineapple and cut the tender part of the flesh into 1/2-inch pieces.

Place the pineapple pieces and Grand Marnier liqueur in a bowl and toss the pieces to coat them. Refrigerate for at least 1 hour to allow the pineapple to absorb as much of the liqueur as possible.

In a large bowl, whip the egg whites with the sugar until the whites become firm. Add the mascarpone to the egg whites and sugar. Delicately whisk the mixture together until the texture reaches that of heavy cream. Add the pineapple pieces to the mascarpone and toss to coat them evenly.

Divide the pineapple among four chilled parfait glasses and garnish each serving with the green leaves. Serve chilled.

FLAMING CAFÉ TRINIDAD

A friend of mine and I were once trading stories about great restaurant desserts. "One of my fond memories of the Los Feliz Inn," the friend said, "was finishing a luxurious lunch with a cup of their Flaming Café Trinidad." It's a perfect combination of a coffee-dessert with a kick.

FOR EACH GLASS OF CAFÉ TRINIDAD

	hot coffee	1/2 ounce	crème de cacao or coffee liqueur
1 piece	thin sliced orange peel, about 1/2 inch wide by 3 inches long	1/2 ounce	good brandy
			whipped cream
1 1/2 ounces	Grand Marnier liqueur	1 small	sugar cube, soaked in brandy

Slowly pour hot coffee into a large-size dessert glass with a short stem until the glass is half full. Twist a slice of orange peel to add the orange oil and zest to the coffee. Add the Grand Marnier, crème de cacao and brandy.

Add more coffee to bring cup to almost full.

Place a spoonful of whipped cream on top

In a teaspoon, place the sugar cube soaked in brandy and balance it on top of the whipped cream. Flame the soaked sugar cube and serve.

The Los Feliz Inn, which stood on Hillhurst Avenue for almost 30 years before closing, featured a traditional country inn feeling and fine-quality dining.

The Inn was known for serving outstanding food cooked with love by chef Pierre Pelech, who owned the restaurant with Ron Erickson.

Los Feliz Inn was in its heyday when prime rib was still a favorite Los Angeles dinner entrée but the restaurant also pioneered the serving of fresh fish in its Mediterranean-style dishes long before healthful eating and exercise gained prominence.

Flaming favorites were a signature as well. The fresh spinach salad was flambéed tableside as was this Flaming Café Trinidad for dessert.

Recipe courtesy of Laurie Burrows Grad,
Dining in Los Angeles

Of the many ethnic restaurants found in Los Angeles, Xiomara stands out as showcase of traditional Cuban fare. The charming and petite owner, Xiomara Ardolina, can be found there monitoring the kitchen and the dining room guiding the guests to the best dining choice for the evening.

Cuban-born Ardolino moved to the United States when she was 13 and became exposed to varied styles of Cuban cooking in Miami and New York.

Having opened other restaurants, Xiomara used this background to refine her Cuban home-cooking in the direction of Neuvo Latino. Her dishes also contain French and even Chinese influences.

Xiomara's interior is charming, with a staircase to a second level and a wrought-iron balcony overlooking the Havana-style mahogany bar and main dining room. A seat next to this balcony is perfect for viewing the activity below.

A specialty cocktail, the Xiomara Mambo, is a mojito given a secret twist by adding freshly squeezed sugar cane juice, lots of mint and lime. Also not to be missed are such other specialties as the classic black bean soup, the Cuban tamales over lobster bisque, and seared pork hash and shredded duck.

XIOMARA
FROZEN KEY LIME SOUFFLÉ

Here is a light, refreshing dessert using the tart juice of key limes. The addition of meringue and coconut toffee sauce add an elegant touch.

YIELD: 8 SERVINGS

1 1/2 teaspoons	powdered gelatin	5 large	egg yolks (reserve 3 of the egg whites for the meringue topping)
1/4 cup	water		
3/4 cup	heavy cream, whipped	1 14 ounce can	condensed milk
1 1/2 cups	lime juice		

Brush eight 4-ounce ramekins with oil or line them with plastic wrap for removal at serving time.

In a small bowl, sprinkle the gelatin over the water and let it stand until softened, about 5 minutes.

Whip the cream and set it aside.

In a heavy saucepan, reduce the lime juice by half (3/4 cup) and whisk in the egg yolks. Cook over moderate low heat, whisking constantly, until it is boiling and thickened, about 5 minutes. Remove the mixture from heat and add the gelatin, condensed milk and whipped cream. Mix well.

Place a coconut cookie or other cookie in the bottom of each ramekin, then fill each with some of the soufflé mixture. Allow the soufflés to freeze.

MERINGUE TOPPING

3 large	egg whites	1cup	sugar

Place the egg whites in a medium-to-large bowl over simmering water to warm them. Then with an electric mixer, whip the egg whites until they have formed soft peaks. Slowly add the sugar to the whites, mixing continuously until sugar is completely dissolved.

Place the meringue in a pastry bag for piping onto the top of soufflé.

COCONUT TOFFEE SAUCE

1 cup	coconut milk (thick)	1 teaspoon	unsalted butter
1/4 cup	whole milk	1/2 teaspoon	vanilla
1/3 cup	granulated sugar		Pinch salt

In a saucepan, combine the coconut and whole milks, the sugar, butter and salt and cook the mixture until the liquid is reduced by half. Remove from heat, add vanilla and allow the mixture to cool.

FOR ASSEMBLY

Remove the soufflés from the ramekins, turning the ramekins upside down on a dish. (The cookie should be on top). Pipe about 2 to 3 tablespoons of the meringue on top of each soufflé and torch the meringue to lightly brown it. When serving, surround each soufflé with about 2 tablespoons of the coconut toffee sauce.

STRAWBERRIES ROMANOFF

Michael Romanoff was a Lithuanian-born restaurateur and self-proclaimed member of Russian royalty. His Beverly Hills restaurant was a celebrity hangout for Hollywood stars during the 1940s and 1950s, before it closed on New Year's Eve in 1962. This dessert was said to be a favorite of Romanoff's customers, especially when fresh strawberries were in season.

YIELD: 8 SERVINGS

1/4 cup	strawberry liqueur	2 tablespoons	dark brown sugar
1/4 cup	orange liqueur, preferably Grand Marnier or Cointreau	2 baskets	fresh strawberries
2 tablespoons	cognac	3 pints	French-vanilla ice cream
	juice from 1 lemon	1 cup	whipped cream

In a large bowl, combine the strawberry and orange liqueurs, cognac, lemon juice and up to 2 tablespoons of brown sugar, depending on sweetness of berries and lemon juice.

Rinse the strawberries, and set aside 8 whole ones for garnish. Hull and halve the remaining strawberries, then marinate the halves in the liqueur mixture for about 15 minutes.

In a large bowl, soften 2 pints of the vanilla ice cream, then fold in the whipped cream. Fold in the marinated strawberry mixture.

Place a small scoop of the remaining 1 pint of ice cream in each of eight large stemmed glasses. Fill the glasses with the ice-cream-strawberry mixture, then garnish each with one of the reserved whole berries. Sprinkle each serving with additional brown sugar to taste, if desired. Serve at once.

Californians love their fresh, home grown fruit and strawberries are no exception. This wholesome, delicately flavored berry is grown year-round in California. This is why desserts featuring the red, juicy little fruit are a popular addition to any menu. Romanoff's complements this strawberry and cream mixture with a little Grand Marnier to wake up the taste buds. A sprinkle of brown sugar before serving puts Romanoff's version over the top.

Recipe courtesy of Ruth Dosti
Dear S.O.S – 30 Years of Recipe Requests to the L.A. Times

PIE CRUST

12 tablespoons	unsalted butter, chilled
4 tablespoons	vegetable shortening, chilled
2 1/2 cup	all-purpose flour, plus extra for rolling dough
1 teaspoon	salt
4 to 6 tablespoons	ice water

Cut the butter and shortening into 1/2-inch cubes.

Sift the flour and salt into a food processor. Add the butter and pulse several times until the mixture looks like coarse crumbs. Add the shortening and pulse another 3 to 4 times. Add 1 to 2 tablespoons of ice water and pulse until the mixture holds together when pressed. Add another 1 to 2 tablespoons of water as necessary until dough comes together. Be careful not to over-mix. (The dough may also be mixed using a pastry cutter for cutting the butter and shortening into the flour and salt, and blending the dough into pea-size pieces.)

Squeeze the dough into two round disks. Wrap them in plastic wrap and refrigerate for a minimum of 30 minutes.

Remove the dough from the refrigerator, and place it on a floured work surface. With a rolling pin, roll the dough into an 11-inch circle and press it into a 9-inch pie pan. Use the same procedure to create the top of the pie.

CHOCOLATE SAUCE

YIELD: 1 1/4 CUPS

3/4 cup	heavy cream
1 cup	semi-sweet chocolate chips
1/2 tablespoon	unsalted butter

Place the chocolate chips in a medium-size bowl. In a small saucepan, heat the cream, being careful not to boil it. Pour the cream over chocolate chips and stir until the chocolate is melted. Stir in butter until blended.

Serve as topping over your favorite dessert.

Whiskey Sauce

YIELD: 1 CUP

	yolks from 3 large eggs
1/4 cup	sugar
1/2 cup	heavy cream
1 teaspoon	unsalted butter
1/2 teaspoon	vanilla
2 tablespoons	whiskey

In a medium-size bowl, whisk the egg yolks and sugar until the sugar is dissolved and the yolks are a pale yellow. Set aside.

In a medium-size saucepan, heat the cream and butter until the cream boils. Remove from heat and add 1 to 2 tablespoons of the egg yolk and sugar mixture and whisk to incorporate. Add the remaining egg-yolk mixture to the cream and butter and heat, stirring constantly until the mixture thickens, about 3 to 5 minutes. Add the vanilla and whiskey and stir to combine. Strain the sauce to remove any small lumps that may have appeared.

The sauce may be served warm or cool and is typically used as a topping for bread puddings.

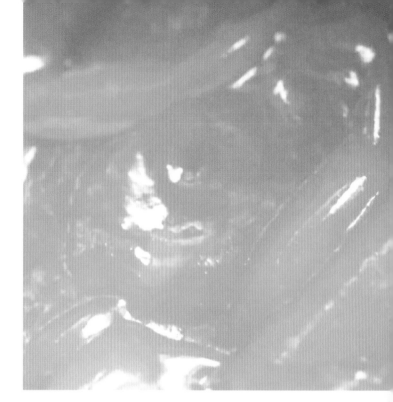

Mint Tea

4 cups	water
4 teaspoons	green tea
2 tablespoons	granulated sugar
20	mint leaves, lightly crushed, plus extra for garnish

Pre-warm the tea pot by pouring in 1 cup of boiling water and let sit for 2 to 4 minutes.

Pour the water out of the pot.

In a saucepan, bring the 4 cups of water to a boil.

Place the green tea, sugar, and mint leaves in the teapot, add the boiled water and stir to combine the ingredients. Allow to steep for 2 to 3 minutes. Using a fine-mesh strainer, pour the tea into the desired number of cups. Add a sprig of mint to each cup for garnish.

Serve immediately.

BAKING ESSENTIALS

Our pastry chef advisors emphasized that the proper tools and ingredients are essential. Consequently, the following are the items we collected and returned to most often to prepare these recipes. They will stir you to success.

Aluminum foil
Baker's parchment
Baker's sugar, extra fine
Baking powder
Baking sheets, best quality
Baking soda
Butane kitchen torch
Cake cooling racks
Cake pans, 8" and 9", 2 to 4 of each
Cake rounds, cardboard circles
Candy thermometer
Cane syrup
Cheese grater, small grate
Chinois
Chocolate, Baker's unsweetened
Chocolate, dark
Chocolate, milk
Chocolate, semi-sweet
Chocolate, white
Cinnamon grated
Cinnamon sticks
Citrus peeler
Citrus zester
Cocoa powder
Colander
Condensed milk, sweetened
Confectioners' sugar
Cookbook stand, acrylic
Corn syrup, dark
Corn syrup, light
Counter stand electric mixer
Dry yeast
Espresso powder
Evaporated milk
Eye dropper
Fire extinguisher
Flour, all-purpose
Flour, self-rising
Glass mixing bowls, assortment
Granulated sugar
Hand mixer, electric
Icing spreader, crooked blade
Icing spreader, flat blade
Kitchen towels, 1 to 2 dozen
Knife sharpener
Knives, assortment, excellent quality
Ladles, small, medium & large

Marble slab, 2- foot x 3- foot
Matte knife
Measuring cups set: dry
Measuring cups set: liquid
Measuring spoons, two sets
Music
Oven-proof baking bags
Paint brush, artist's small
Pam spray, unflavored
Paper towels
Pastry bag with decorative tips
Pastry cutter
Patience
Pen, pencil
Pennies, pound
Pie server
Plastic binder for recipes & notes
Plastic wrap
Pyrex pie pans
Ramekins
Rolling pin
Rubber spatulas, various sizes
Ruler
Scissors
Serving dishes & platters, assortment
Sifter
Small bowls, assortment
Spatula
Squeeze bottle, small tip
Stainless steel mixing bowls:
Storage containers with lids
Strainer, small, medium & large mesh
Sugar, dark brown
Sugar, light brown
Tart tins
Timer
Tongs, small and large
Toothpicks, long
Unsalted butter
Vanilla, beans
Vanilla, pure extract, best quality
Vegetable oil
Vegetable peeler
Waxed paper
Whisks, small, medium & large
Wooden chopping block
Wooden spoons, assortment

INDEX

ACKNOWLEDGEMENTS

"None is more impoverished than the one who has no gratitude. Gratitude is a currency that we can mint for ourselves, and spend without fear of bankruptcy."

–Fred De Witt Van Amburgh

There are lots of 'hands in the pot' as far as production of a dessert and of a book. I am especially thankful to those who helped make this possible. I am grateful to my daughter Allison Meyerson for creative photography and for her patience accommodating baking schedules. Mark Meyerson was counted on for photo assisting.

I owe a debt of gratitiude to the pastry chefs who made this book possible.

Thanks to Michael Lauve for his work as art director evidenced throughout.

Special thanks to Kit Wohl for designing and creating the original Classic Desserts book and who became my mentor and guide. And, thanks to Billy Wohl who supported Kit in this process.

Chef Robert Barker helped save the day when mousses wouldn't gel or crepes fell apart. Zach Engel lent a hand in the kitchen and dessert plating.

Thanks to Milburn Calhoun at Pelican Publishing for asking me to write this book; and to Nina Kooij, John Scheyd, Katie Szadiewicz, and Terry Callaway for supporting the process and to the book sellers who move the process along.

I'm grateful to Gene Bourg and Christine Ziemba for checking and reviewing what I wrote.

I am indebted to Kathleen Bergstrom and Jenninfer Evans Gardner for taking time to advise and guide me toward understanding some of the Los Angeles culinary landscape.

Leah, and Kate, my daughters patiently read the recipes and notes and offered unbiased advice throughout. Thanks to my son, Mac Bauer who lent his encouragement when I simply couldn't imagine preparing another dessert.

And to Eleanor Roemer and Barbara Spangenberg for their friendship and encouragement.

Special thanks to my grandchildren GraceRose Bauer, Zander and Jasper Meyerson who were the best dessert 'tasters' anyone could have.

For any errors or omissions, I take responsibility.

Comments are invited, send to gracebauer07@gmail.com.